Waldheim

Waldheim

Bernard Cohen

Luc Rosenzweig

translated by Josephine Bacon

Adama Books

New York

First published in French under the title *Le Mystère Waldheir*
© *Editions Gallimard*, 1986. Translated by Josephine Bacon

Library of Congress Cataloging-in-Publication Data

Cohen, Bernard, 1956 or 7–
   Waldheim. *47709*
   Translation of: Le mystère Waldheim.
   1. Waldheim, Kurt. 2. Austria—Presidents—
Biography. 3. United Nations. Secretary-General—
Biography. I. Rosenzweig, Luc. II. Title.
DB98.W28C6413 1987 943.6′053′0924 [B] 87-19276
ISBN 1-557-74010-0

Printed in Israel
Design by Jane Brenner
Composition by Ari Davidow and Associates
Cover design by Irwin Rosenhouse

Adama Books, 306 West 38 Street, New York, NY 10018

Acknowledgements

Our investigation into the Waldheim affair benefited from the friendly and efficient cooperation of many people who showed their confidence by providing us with valuable assistance.

The following must be graciously thanked: Mrs Ruth Valentini of the *Nouvel Observateur*, through whom we were able to obtain Kurt Waldheim's doctoral thesis. Mr. Alain Navarro, an *Agence France-Presse* journalist in Jerusalem and Mr. Denis Scribe, the *Libération* correspondent in Athens, also facilitated our task. In Vienna, where many Austrian friends helped us to understand the complexity of this ancient land, particular thanks are due to Mr. Georg Hoffman-Ostenhof, leader writer of the *Arbeiterzeitung* and Mr. Michel Cullin, former Director of the French Institute in Vienna.

There are many more, who wish to remain anonymous, who were kind enough to give us exclusive interviews, despite the fact that they hold important positions throughout the world.

Translator's Note

The translator would like to thank the librarians at the Wiener Library, London.

Wherever possible, quotations from material which originally appeared in English have been copied from the original source, but this has not always been possible. Where the original was in neither English nor French, an English translation has generally been made from the French version, even where an English edition has been published, since there was not always time to trace the English translation.

Contents

Introduction:
The Duty of Memory

THE story about to be unfolded here does not portray an unusual man, an exceptional individual. On the contrary, it features someone who could be considered to be the embodiment of what Robert Musil[1] has termed "the Austrian national philosophy: dreary routine." Kurt Waldheim passed through the century with his rather self-conscious bearing of the model civil servant, carefully perfecting with a very old world meticulousness the career which led him to the Presidency in the *Alte Hofburg* palace in Vienna. He was a diplomat by nature, not one of the great, daring and agile variety, but more the type whose painstaking effort smooths the rough edges, a preoccupation with which a bureaucrat could spend his whole life.

Nothing ought to have focused prolonged attention on Kurt Waldheim, not even during the ten years he spent at the head of the United Nations (UN). When the post of UN Secretary-General fell to his lot in 1972, the great powers had decided to offer it to a personality without personality, who would run the international community like a government department, combining coldness with flexibility, a distant demeanor with innate opportunism. When he returned to dealing with Austrian affairs of state, Kurt Waldheim never attempted to descend into the political arena and become federal chancellor; no one even asked him to do so. No, this man with his penchant for amassing honors needed a post which would reflect the rather tarnished glory of the Austro-Hungarian Empire, and in 1986, that happened to be his successful race for the Presidency. Then the scandal broke, and it was all the more spectacular since it affected a zealous diplomat who was both accommodating and colorless. Paradoxically, a new kind of man was about to accede to the highest office Austria had to offer.

Waldheim now is a totally different character than the man the public knew through the preceding three decades, especially during the period he spent as Secretary-General of the United Nations, an institution theoretically created to prevent the world from once more committing crimes of state and other forms of genocide. Between one Waldheim and the other lies the space of a campaign, a counterpoint to the candidate's electoral campaign for the presidency of Austria; this was the campaign for the truth, managed from New York by the World Jewish Congress, the main activist in the investigation into the Nazi past of this same Waldheim. Suddenly, the former spokesman of the international community, this future head of state, was found to have been guilty of persistent and repeated lying, those lies compounded by his stubborn denials.

Yet on looking back, the term "scandal" seems inappropriate. The regurgitation of Waldheim's past caused a sensation and media agitation, but did not trouble any consciences, except those of a few Austrians and lovers of historical veracity throughout the world. Many questions may have arisen in people's minds when a 40-year-old deception surfaced like an old print that had been forgotten in a photochemical bath. What did this man really do? How did Austria itself deal with the triumph of Nazism? And could Kurt Waldheim have been a double or triple agent after the war, slipping in and out of Vienna's nostalgic shadows?

However, the most important question which arises, one fraught with suspicion, innuendo and a very palpable unease is why, in 1986—neither before nor after, but at this particular time, which was too fortuitous to be coincidental— why at this particular moment was it recalled that Kurt Waldheim did not spend World War II harmlessly, and that his bland personality concealed a most interesting fate? This question will not be avoided, but it should be stated at the outset that in itself it has served as an alibi, as an expertly-contrived protective screen against all the political, historical and ethical teachings which the Waldheim case ought to exemplify. In fact, in its own way, the question of the timing has even helped to perpetuate the Waldheim lie, because as long as there is a preoccupation with the question of why Kurt Waldheim's military career in the Third Reich's army was suddenly remembered, it is all too easy to ignore the reasons why it had not been remembered earlier. It is as if, toward the end of this century, memory had become so unreliable that before it could testify at the tribunal of history, it had to be submitted to a morality investigation (of a type to which Kurt Waldheim, honorable Austrian diplomat that he was, had never been subjected when he became head of the United Nations Organization). In any event, Vietnam, Cambodia and other traumatic events had long since disbanded this court of justice which 20 years previously had been haunted by intellectuals with grave delight.

The Kurt Waldheim affair could even be interpreted as a Viennese tale of memory tricks and deceptions.

Waldheim has emerged as less suspect than his accusers. He, at least, had a clear motive, and in the frustrating political situation in which the West finds itself today, a bad motive is better than none at all. The inglorious career of Kurt Waldheim would never have attracted worldwide attention had it not eventually challenged everyone and asked the question of the world at large: "What is the point of remembering?"

The tiny silver spoons in the *Kunsthistorisches* Museum in Vienna, which once belonged to the Empress Maria Theresa, have been religiously preserved. As recently as summer, 1986, a diplomat attached to the Austrian embassy in Bern, Switzerland discreetly emerged from the Geneva morgue with a package under his arm. The package was sent back immediately to his own country through official channels. It contained a beaker of formaldehyde in which the head had been preserved of the Italian anarchist, Luigi Lucheni, who on September 10, 1898 stabbed the Empress Elisabeth of Austria. Such a pathological attachment to the past does not usually provoke criticism. Yet the fact is that no one considered it intolerable that a man who aspired to the presidency of Austria had camouflaged his responsibility from 1939 to 1945, while here was this trivial preoccupation with some insignificant relic of the past. Perhaps, a century later, there are some Austrian officials who still dream of finding the chromosome of crime inside Lucheni's brain, which for so long preoccupied the minds of the more credulous dabblers in science. Yet there was little desire to learn anything about far more recent skeletons in the cupboard, namely the obsession with concealment of the truth about World War II which typifies the Waldheim case.

Austria does not bear the burden of amnesia alone. The controversy unleashed by Kurt Waldheim's faked biography has probably given Europe its last chance to attempt a critical review, remote from the passions aroused by the Liberation, of that period during which Western values degenerated into barbarism. Europe has declined to make use of it, partly from ignorance, but mainly from shame, and—at least as far as the world leaders are concerned—from cowardice. Robert Paxton and Michael Marrus, who have studied the origins of collaboration in France,[2] have lifted the veil and suggested that the silence which has penetrated the deepest recesses of the national conscience is in danger of smothering it. This demand for the truth disquiets the older nations even more than does their own retreat into a sclerotic forgetfulness, or even their fictitious rewriting.

Within the space of a few months, Europe had exhibited multiple symptoms of this delirious amnesia, comparable to the uneasy doze that follows a badly digested meal. At the very time when Klaus Barbie, "Butcher of Lyons", was being remanded in custody by a judicial procedure whose slowness mocked the very concept of delayed punishment, several former Nazis (such as the Belgian, Leon Degrelle) were living a life of ease and freedom in Spain, though their former hosts, the Franco regime, had long since been cast into oblivion. At the same time, the East German authorities were calmly contemplating the construction in East Berlin of a freeway which would have involved the destruction of the largest Jewish cemetery in Europe. The former British Prime Minister, Harold Macmillan (now Lord Stockton), had the magazine of his own party's youth organization, *New Agenda*, suppressed because it repeated the accusation that during the war he delivered 40,000 Cossacks and White Russians to Stalinist repression.

The epidemic of these sinister attempts to deny a recent past almost too terrible to contemplate appears to have spread throughout the West. The vectors have been men with genuine academic qualifications, who have devoted their intellectual abilities to 'proving' that the Holocaust and its attendant horrors never even took place. These revisionist historians include the French professor Robert Faurisson and his eager pupil Henri Roques who was awarded his doctorate on the basis of this very thesis (he even got a very good grade!), David Irving in Great Britain, and in the U.S., Professor A.R. Butz (albeit a professor of engineering!) of Northwestern University who wrote *The Hoax of the Twentieth Century*—the hoax in question being the Nazi Holocaust. There are many other examples of this type of obscene rewriting of history in the United States, many of them published by the notorious Institute for Historical Review in Torrance, California.

Founded in 1978 by Willis A. Carto the institute publishes the authoritative-sounding *Journal of Historical Review*. There are numerous other authorities writing and lecturing, all of them ultimately funded by the American Nazi party and other groups, who are busy claiming that Hitler's war was a justifiable reaction to Jewish aggression.

In much the same vein, a West German medical authority recently suggested tattooing a number on the forearms of AIDS carriers, in terrifying mimicry of those who once sought to track down the ideological contamination of Jews and homosexuals.

Amnesia has certainly won the day, doubtless because the generations who were spared World War II have allowed themselves to be overwhelmed by a blanket scepticism of contemporary history, due largely to the existence of too much written material heavily laced with ulterior motives and self-justifications.

As an example, Alexandre de Marenches, a former head of the French information services, tells how one day, while visiting the cellars of the SDECE, the French intelligence and counter-intelligence branch, he came across a ten ton pile of archive material, "bundled together, all piled in a mess." This was in 1970. He then learned that these were Gestapo and Abwehr (German Intelligence) documents which had been seized during the Liberation. At first, he tried to put them into some semblance of order, but eventually he gave up. "I pulled out a few documents at random. The result was unpleasant, even painful. There were prominent men of today who had been or had claimed to have been members of the resistance and true patriots. In reality, they had been in the pay of the Germans. I considered at the time, and still do, that since one of the most pernicious of French vices is divisiveness, we do not need—since these people are still alive—to go rummaging around in trash cans and stirring up the dirt, not to put too fine a point on it."[3]

The fact that the West has learned to conceal the past from itself has naturally contributed to the sowing of confusion among those nations who gained their independence after World War II, and who have no spontaneous desire to conduct a critical survey of history. Those who were primarily involved refuse to undertake this problem themselves. The Arab world, for the most part, believed at the time that the confrontation between the Allies and the Axis would toll the death knell of Western domination and restore the lost glory of the ancient Islamic conquest. For many Arab intellectuals, it was not a case of supporting right or wrong, but of rallying to the strongest while awaiting the final death. The ethical element in the fight against Nazism was not clear.

Here is an obviously extreme but nonetheless eloquent example. Muammar el Qaddafi explained one day to American journalists how Ronald Reagan had come to work for the *Mossad*, Israel's secret service. "He became an Israeli agent because he had been in the Gestapo and wanted to conceal his past," claimed the Libyan colonel in a syllogism which is as unmatched as it is disturbing.[4] The romance between the martyr and his executioner ends in the total inversion of roles, along a path of history trodden by characters in fancy dress. Thus, ever since his accession to the Presidency of Austria, Kurt Waldheim has been showered with messages of congratulation and cordial invitations from Colonel Qaddafi, dignitaries of the Khomeini regime in Iran, and Syrian President Hafez Al-Assad.

Now that the latter part of the century seems to be degenerating into an unprecedented confrontation between an aging West and a Third World which has become so radicalized as to lose its bearings entirely, it would be all too easy to incriminate Kurt Waldheim's Arab sympathizers. All the Western countries, even Israel, in a deliberate way, have shown a suspect complacency with regard to this man whose career under the Third Reich we shall attempt to trace here. The fact that no country has shown any intention of reviving the purely legal aspect of the affair—Kurt Waldheim is still technically subject to a request for extradition for war crimes issued by Yugoslavia in 1947—is understandable; justice is always meted out sparingly to the great men of this world. Yet no democracy, however convinced of the transparency of its institutions, has dared to disapprove of the election of a candidate who only a few days prior to his victory had submitted a biography which was indisputably fake.

Respect for Austrian sovereignty has been invoked to justify this troubled silence. Yet isn't the sovereignty of the democratic conscience just as respectable? After each hijacking, after each assassination attempt, all the editorialists in Paris, London and New York indignantly note that the rule of human decency chosen by the greatest number can be dragged through the mud by a handful of freedom fighters. Yet to whom should such lessons be addressed if the democracies themselves no longer believe in their most basic principles?

The Austrians elected Kurt Waldheim as a purely nationalistic reflex (and, as a secondary consideration, as a warning to the Socialists who were then in power). "We ourselves shall choose whoever we want," proclaimed Kurt Waldheim under the banner of an electoral program which enabled him to evade any serious discussion of his past which was then under review. This qualifies him to enter the ranks of a very old political tradition. Even an ancient one. Nearly a century ago, a Spanish demagogue, Antonio Maura, conducted his campaign purely on the slogan, *"Nosotros somos nosotros"*—"We are who we are." The God of the Bible may have been able to introduce himself in this way, but not so a professional politician. Yet Kurt Waldheim allowed himself this luxury because he knew he was being protected by a double silence, that of the Austrian people and that of the Western nations.

If there is such a thing as a Waldheim mystery, it lies primarily in this tacit complicity. It is not too arduous a task for the conscientious historian to retrace step by step the lives of the major Nazi war criminals. But to follow the week-by-week activities of a German intelligence officer in the maelstrøm of the Balkans requires another kind of energy, and even a different approach to contemporary history. It is no longer a matter, as was too often the case after the war, of using a few human monsters to exorcise the Nazi trauma, but to understand, 40 years later, how anonymous citizens could have permitted the machine to operate through their excessive zeal and defective consciences.

To deny that Kurt Waldheim had been able to choose a different course of action during those dramatic days, as Ronald Reagan himself has not hesitated to suggest ("Like thousands of German soldiers, he did his duty," the President informed the daily newspaper *USA Today*), eventually means forbidding any initiative of freedom of choice, and despising the crucial moment at which the need for liberty is paramount. This means the freedom to reject barbarism yesterday, and the freedom to know about it today; respect for these two requirements demands that the Waldheim case should not remain a simple affair, and should not merely be allowed to swell the ranks of those depressing anecdotes which make the average newspaper reader exclaim, "Oh well. Politicians are all the same."

Kurt Waldheim has been warmly saluted by the terrorist Abu Nidal, and was under investigation by the US Department of Justice. He has been indicted in Yugoslavia but absolved in Greece. By now he ought to have acquired the international dimension he sought after leaving his post as head of the United Nations, when the limelight of the world's press was focused on him. That is why research into the hidden truths and deceptions which surrounded him had to be conducted in New York, Belgrade, Helsinki, Jerusalem, Athens and Vienna.

There are still some countries which do not want to shed more light on this global intrigue. Italy, for instance, whose leaders have been approached by various investigators, claims to be unable to overcome the problem of the confusion of its war archives. As for the protagonist himself, who was so quick to grant interviews during his electoral campaign, he has rejected the offer by the Bertrand Russell International Court to hold a meeting of experts in Vienna to review his past.

This silence has been widely applauded, not only by nations, but even by private individuals. The evidence lies in the vast amount of mail which the two authors received while they were reporting this matter for their respective newspapers, *Libération* and *Le Monde*. There were threats of various degrees of violence, insults, references to their Jewish-sounding names, reference to plots.

Is Waldheim such a mystery? Of course, the reconstitution of his murky and obscure past sometimes takes on the air of a detective story. But nothing here smacks of the fictional. Police forces only act on orders. The attempt to penetrate the web of silence and deceit has mainly involved watching a world which does not want to remember. In his long-winded autobiographies,[5] Kurt Waldheim had the material for the story of the century, had he wanted to tell it. He could have told of the collapse of old empires, the deceptive triumph of Nazi brutality, the compromises of postwar European reconstructionism, the manipulation of third world aspirations to independence, the inexorable decline of the institutions of international joint action, the senile return to the chauvinist creed of the European nations.

Immediately after the election, when Kurt Waldheim realized that his first problem would be his inability to make official visits abroad without constantly reawakening the controversy, he sought to take advantage of an invitation from the Republic of Ireland issued to his presidential predecessor. During World War II, Ireland had opted for neutrality; Eamon de Valera, the great advocate of neutrality, had no objection to paying homage to Hitler when the death of the

Führer was announced. Full of coincidence and surprises, Kurt Waldheim's career is stamped with a remarkably consistent refrain, the refrain of international compromise.

1
The Origins
of an Opportunist

*A man without qualities consists
of qualities without a man.*
Robert Musil

THE road that runs from Tulln, a little town in Lower Austria, to Vienna, the city of Sigmund Freud and Arthur Schnitzler, is quite short, barely 25 miles long. It follows the Danube to Klosterneuburg, then plunges among the vineyards and meadows typical of the rolling Austrian countryside where the Viennese spend their weekends. Once upon a time, this was the last stage of the route linking the two great cities of the Austro-Hungarian Empire, Prague and Vienna. Perhaps it was from fear of confronting the capital that Kurt Waldheim's ancestors, Moravian peasants in search of prosperity, remained in this region. In fact, Vaclaviks found employment there. These emigrants had much in common with the wine-growers of the region; they shared the Roman Catholicism of the countryside, larded with ancient superstitions and a pride in being loyal subjects of the Emperor Franz Josef.

In leaving Moravia and settling in the German part of the Empire, the Vaclaviks had embarked on the course taken by millions in that mosaic of nations united under the authority of the dual monarchy. This was the route to assimilation and the rejection of ethnic origins, Czech, Hungarian, Jewish, in order to benefit from assimilation into a state where the entrance ticket was either baptism or, where this was unnecessary, the eradication of any trace of Slavism. Even today, Kurt Waldheim prefers not to talk about his ancestors.

All of Waldheim's biographers have been surprised at how disinclined he has been to expand on his youth and his family background. Before the news spotlight was focused on him, encouraging journalists and publicists to delve into every corner of his life, this reticence was attributed to the natural reserve of a rather introverted individual, who had been practicing diplomacy too long. Others were less generous. One of his closest co-workers, who is still active in New York, says of him, "He is stupidly pretentious, and so egocentric that he believes the merest banality uttered by the UN Secretary-

General must change the face of the earth." This man still remembers with displeasure the time he spent correcting a copy of a book of interviews which Kurt Waldheim had given to the French journalist Eric Rouleau.[6] "Anything he said that might have been in any way vivid, spontaneous, personal had to be erased, leaving only those passages that were the most insipid and platitudinous."

Yet the history of the Vaclavik-Waldheim family is by no means devoid of interest. It could even be cited as a classic example of the Austrian experience in this century, where only the capacity for individual survival, family unity, and a fierce desire to succeed prevented people from sinking into decadence and despair.

Kurt Waldheim's grandfather was a blacksmith. His father, Walter, became an elementary school teacher just before World War I. The family still bore the name Vaclavik. Shortly before Kurt was born, on December 21, 1918, Walter Vaclavik decided to break the last ties to Czechoslovakia, a country that had become independent since the defeat of the Empire, so he consequently abandoned the family surname. During the 1986 electoral campaign, his son recalled the reason which had made his father climb the last rung on the ladder to total Germanization, "During World War I, my father, who was a much-decorated officer, was wounded. The Czech doctor at the military hospital refused to treat him because he did not speak Czech. . . ."

Germanization of the Vaclaviks

THIS anecdote may well be true: the disintegration of the imperial army at the end of the war had created tensions. The recently-liberated nations took their revenge for centuries of political and cultural oppression. Yet, typically, Kurt

Waldheim gives only one version of events in public, the one which fits in with the idyllic image he tries to depict of his personal and family past. In any case, before being confronted with the evidence of his origins—about which there is nothing in the least shameful—he used to pretend, at fashionable receptions and embassy cocktail parties, that he was the product of an upper class Austrian family which had certain aristocratic connections....

As far as Walter Vaclavik was concerned, the end of the war meant that he had to try and assure a precarious living for his growing family. He had long been active in the Christian Social Party, so he took the advice of his friend, Alois Reiter, who was then Chairman of the Regional Council of the province of Lower Austria, who told him that with his Bohemian last name, he'd never get anywhere. Walter did not need telling twice. The population register was then administered exclusively by the church. Walter Vaclavik applied and took the necessary steps to change his name. The new family name chosen, Waldheim, is worth a closer look. It consists of two words: *Wald*, wood or forest, and *Heim*, home. These are the two foundations of the German soul. Invoking them fills even the most hardened German heart with emotion.

Did Walter Vaclavik-Waldheim have a premonition at the time that one of his sons would seek the votes of his fellow citizens to become President of the Republic of Austria? Whether he did or not, no public relations firm could have dreamed up a better name: The name is a whole electoral program in itself, in a country where attachment to the soil, the wearing of national dress, three-piece suits of grey-green *loden* cloth and the plumed hat, can win more votes than pretty speeches. Former Chancellor Bruno Kreisky, whose family could boast of having lived in Vienna for many centuries, needed all his political acumen to ward off the base attacks of his opponents in the People's Party made on the basis of his Jewish origins.

In 1970, that party, which was to be the main supporter of Kurt Waldheim's candidacy, fought Bruno Kreisky who was then the ascendant. Their candidate was the outgoing Chancellor, Josef Klaus, and their slogan, "Vote for a genuine Austrian," was a broad hint that their candidate's opponent, who had never denied his Jewish roots, could not himself lay claim to such genuineness. "And this was actually the least offensive of the type of insinuations that were being made at the time. I was being attacked in a much more directly anti-Semitic way by members of Parliament of the People's Party during that electoral campaign," the retired Chancellor recalled 16 years later.

So that's how, immediately after World War I, Walter Vaclavik became an Austrian with a genuine surname in a country which liked to call itself *Deutschösterreich*, German Austria, in contrast to those parts of the Empire that had won their independence and national identity, i.e., Czechoslovakia, Hungary and Yugoslavia. This new identity was no disadvantage to the young teacher. Quite the contrary. He soon became a headmaster, then in 1928, when young Kurt was nearly 10 years old, Walter was made inspector of the Tulln district. The Waldheim family's ideological compass pointed toward Vienna, but not the cosmopolitan Vienna of the progressive political, intellectual and artistic movements whose influence is still strong, the Vienna of the Austrian Marxists Victor Adler and Otto Bauer. They sought a compromise between Bolshevism and Social Democracy. Sigmund Freud, too, was busy inventing psychoanalysis. The mere mention of these names in Tulln was sufficient to make the people cross themselves.

A Fierce Catholicism

In stark contrast, two eminent clerics were active in the capital city to show the true way to those who might have been tempted to stray into the path of secularism. These were the Archbishop of Vienna, Cardinald Karl Dietrich Piffl and a priest, Ignaz Seipel, President of the Christian-Social Party, to which Kurt Waldheim's father belonged. These two churchmen were to stamp their strong personalities on the first Austrian Republic. Cardinal Piffl brought Roman Catholics into acceptance of the new republic. Deeply attached as they were to the royal house, the Austrian Catholic nation in fact disapproved of this new republic, especially as it was headed, for the first time in the history of the country, by a Social-Democrat, Karl Renner, who led a coalition government with the Christian-Social party.

Within the party, the priest, Ignaz Seipel, was Minister of Social Affairs. The Piffl-Seipel tandem succeeded in forcing the Emperor to abdicate and Ignaz Seipel became Chancellor in 1920, after the Social-Democratic withdrawal from the coalition government. For the people of Tulln, peasants and white-collar workers, the *Rotenturmstrasse,* the palace of the archbishops in Vienna, and the chancellory constituted a bastion against "Red Vienna" whose militant suburbs lay almost cheek by jowl with their own green countryside. For 12 years, the Cardinal and the Chancellor succeeded in maintaining a semblance of order in a country where the rift was widening. Their almost simultaneous deaths in 1932 heralded a period of great unrest.

Kurt Waldheim had always wanted to be a man without political affiliations. However, he has never denied belonging to the conservative Christian movement of which the organized sector today constitutes most of the strength of the Austrian People's Party (ÖVP). In fact, after 1945, his career advanced under the protection of the leaders of that political grouping. He owes his entry into the Ministry of Foreign Affairs to Karl Gruber, a genuine Tyrolean resistance member who was one of the founders of the People's Party in 1945. Gruber, and his private secretary, Fritz Molden, tried to give the party a less traditional coloration, one which was directed more toward social Catholicism than its prewar predecessor, the Christian Social party of Engelbert Dollfuss and Kurt von Schuschnigg, whose orientation, despite the name, was resolutely clerical and very conservative. The evolution of the Christian Social party ended, in fact, in 1934 with the setting up under their direction, of the Christian Austrian corporatist state, better known as Austrofascism.

Kurt Waldheim's explicit references to his Roman Catholicism are numerous but vague. The speeches he has made for popular consumption speak of a "minimal Catholic program" consisting of worthy sentiments: the supreme importance of the family, the glorification of work, the virtue of sacrifice. During the last phase of his presidential campaign, another aspect of Christianity made its appearance: that of the forgiveness of sins, naturally such forgiveness to be applied in the first instance to himself and his past. Kurt Waldheim has never displayed any marked taste for theoretical studies, and has never mentioned a guide or inspiration from among the wide spectrum of Christian thought, past and present. Since, throughout his life, he has adapted to whatever trend happened to be dominant in the church in Austria and everywhere else, it is worth examining in detail the influences to which he might have been subjected during his formative years, in order to understand the path he traveled.

By changing its name, the Waldheim family became part of the German nationalist movement which almost totally engulfed the country in the aftermath of World War I. Even the Social-Democratic Party was not immune from this form of Pan-German nationalism and as early as 1918, many of its members wanted Austria to attach itself to the Reich. In 1928, Walter Waldheim, father of Kurt, was an elementary school inspector in Tulln. He was a prominent local figure. His duties led him to socialize with the political elite of the district, entirely dominated by the Christian Social party. Their ties with the Archbishop of Vienna were virtually organic. After all, the Chancellor, Ignaz Seipel, was a priest and a prelate of the church, so in theory at least, he was subject to the authority of Cardinal Piffl. In fact, the two men acted in perfect harmony and where circumstances required it, they shared their roles.

For instance, on July 15, 1927 Chancellor Seipel ordered that a crowd of Social Democrat demonstrators be fired upon. Eighty- nine bodies lay dead on the streets of Vienna; the Cardinal probably had a few words of compassion for the victims, but he did nothing to condemn the priest-chancellor who had declared in parliament, "Do not ask the government anything that might appear as weakness ... there is a time for firmness and a time for clemency...." Some 25,000 Austrian Catholics left the church in protest at the attitude of the "bloodthirsty prelate".

Despite the proximity of the capital, Tulln was spiritually very remote from this tumult. In Tulln, everything was viewed in a simpler light, with an almost Manichean logic. On the one side there were the Red atheists, and on the other the good Austrians who attended mass every Sunday. The Waldheim family belonged to the latter category. They believed one ought to be grateful to Chancellor Seipel, who, by taking drastic measures with the economy, dismissing one official in three, brought the country out of the inflationary abyss it sunk into after the war.

Walter Waldheim had survived the purge, because he could claim that he had three children, Kurt, Walter and

Gerlinde to support. Nor was it a disadvantage in the prevailing situation that he had political connections to the party in power, especially with *Landeshauptmann* Reiter, chairman of the Lower Austria district council. So everything tends to indicate that the dominant ideology in the Waldheim household was one which distilled that of the chancellory and the archbishop, a viewpoint supported and reinforced by the Sunday sermons of the curate of Tulln.

The Founding Ideas of an Existence

THREE elements could be considered characteristic of the body of opinion in Austria during the First Republic. These were suspicion of the democratic system, German nationalism and anti-socialism, and last but not least, anti-Semitism. If by his determined action, Cardinal Piffl had prevented the restoration of the Monarchy in 1918, letting Emperor Charles leave for exile in Madeira, where he died in 1922. This did not signify that the Church had rallied enthusiastically to the parliamentary system which had been installed. Large sectors of Catholic public opinion had an aversion to the new regime.

Although he was always careful not to let himself be dragged into the wake of the very powerful legitimist faction of the Christian Social Party, Cardinal Piffl could not ignore this segment of public opinion. While democratic values were still defended, (awaiting the "proletarian revolution") by the Social Democratic Party, the Cardinal was compelled to fight on two fronts, against the "Reds", but also against those who reproached him for having given up the Empire in exchange for the almost absolute power of the Church. The result was an authoritarian interpretation of the concept of a republic which reached its zenith under the auspices of the two successors to the Seipl-Piffl duo, Chancellor Engelbert Dollfuss and Cardinal Theodor Innitzer.

The slide into a corporate Christian state and toward the enthusiastic reception for Hitler's annexation of Austria in 1938, was the natural decline of an institution which had only chosen the republican option under pressure of events, and had never held sacred the defence of a parliamentary regime, or civil liberties. Cardinal Piffl himself declared "Let Christians serve their fatherland, whatever form of government there is." In those troubled times, the Catholic hierarchy did not contribute to the awakening in a population over which it had enormous influence—outside of Vienna and the big industrial centers such as Linz, the left had virtually no following—of a spirit of resistance to the eventual installation of a dictatorship. So there is no reason to be surprised at the indifference to the fate of the Austrian Republic shown by a younger generation which had been subject to the influence of those who nostalgically regretted the passing of the old order, the adherents of that mythical land of Kakania, so well described by Robert Musil in *The Man without Qualities*. These were the same people who were beginning to become the propagandists for a new order, whose first accents were to be heard not far from the borders of *Deutschösterreich* in the back room of a Munich beerhall.

In the period between the acceptance—in the absence of any other possible solution—of the Treaties of Versailles and Saint-Germain which reduced the German-speaking area of the Hapsburg Empire to a little alpine republic (Vienna held more than one-fifth of the total population) and the enthusiasm of the March days of 1938 when Hitler entered Vienna and transformed the Austrian Republic into an *Ostmark* (Eastern borderland) of the Third Reich, the Austrian church had also ventured into new territory—Pan-Germanism. This was despite the fact that it had originally contributed to the affirmation of an Austrian identity against the partisans of Pan-Germanism.

There were many reasons to justify this attitude from the Catholic point of view. The least important was no doubt by a congenital Austrian wariness of a Prussian-dominated Germany with a Protestant majority, whose arrogance displeased Vienna, and incidentally, Bavaria as well. Although the former subjects of the Hohenzollerns and the Hapsburgs were ready to get together as fellow Germans to face the threats from East and West, they rediscovered their mutual distrust and secular disputes when the threat was temporarily removed. In a unified German Reich the Austrian Catholic church could never have exercised the power it had had under the First Austrian Republic. The unrest in Germany which followed the defeat of 1918 may have frightened the Viennese prelates. On the country's very doorstep, the 1920 Revolution of the Councils of Bavaria sent a chill down the spines of all the right-thinkers on the opposite bank of the Inn River.

The fight against the Reds thus became the top priority of both the Christian Social Party and the Archbishop. Nothing was more feared than an alliance between the Austro-Marxists and their comrades in the German Social Democratic Party, which might constitute a formidable opposition to the priests. So it really didn't matter to them that it was two Social Democrats, Friedrich Ebert and Herbert Noske, who had actually quelled the Spartacist revolt in Berlin in 1919 at the cost of bloodshed. The devil conjured up by the Austrian Catholics was Socialism in all its variations. "Socialism is the modern Antichrist: it is the conscientious duty of all Catholics to fight it," wrote Professor of Theology Franz Zach in 1919. "Why? Because the Social Democrats do not believe in God nor in Christ, because they want to take the churches away from the Catholics and turn them into movie theaters, because they want to abolish all private property and thus undermine the foundations of Christian society, because they want to drive the peasants away with whips from the sacred heritage of their forefathers, because they want to drag children away from their parents and destroy the Christian family, because they are advocates of 'free love'—a morality fit only for prostitutes and pimps."

In the Austrian context of the time, this unequivocal appeal to fight a holy war against the socialists was not confined to exhorting Roman Catholics into an ideological combat against the new Antichrist. The confrontation took a much more direct turn: clerical shock troops were organized into the Patriotic Front and the *Heimwehr.* These Catholic paramilitary forces fought almost daily battles against the *Schutzbund,* the Social Democrat's own paramilitaries. The priority given to the fight against the Reds was soon to produce a reversal of the Catholic attitude to the question of nationalism. On the death of the Prelate Seipel, the Christian Social party replaced him with a tiny little man only 4′10″ tall, Engelbert Dollfuss, whose opponents were quick to dub him *Milli-meternich.** A doctor of the University of Vienna, Theodore Innitzer, replaced Cardinal Piffl as Archbishop of Vienna. Two elements subsequently led the Church to intensify its struggle against socialism.

The Rise of National Socialism in Austria

THE internal situation was characterized primarily by mounting tension between the two camps, which was to culminate in the Social Democrats' attempted coup on February 12, 1934. This had disastrous consequences; the clerical militia

---

*Prince Metternich (1773–1859) was the Austrian statesman and diplomat who was so powerful and influential that, after the fall of Napoleon, he was able to negotiate a restoration of the European monarchies that had ruled Europe prior to the Napoleonic conquests.

won the day, parliament was suspended, the Communist, Social Democratic and National Socialist Parties were banned, and a corporate Christian state was established.

Abroad, Germany was on the point of surrendering body and soul to National Socialism and its Führer, Adolf Hitler, while in the east atheistic Bolshevism was triumphant. The Austrian Church, through the voices of Cardinal Innitzer and his colleagues in all the dioceses of Austria bestowed their blessing on Austro-fascism. A document from the Austrian episcopate dated 1933 is evidence of this involvement: "The Herr Chancellor [Dollfuss] has informed us of his desire to build a Christian Corporatist State along the lines of the encyclical 'Quadragesimo Anno'.[7] We hereby express to him our deepest gratitude for this recognition by the government of the doctrine of the Church on the State and Society, as well as for the close commonality of ideas which exists between the government and the church represented by the Episcopate...." This meant that any Austrian Roman Catholic who disassociated himself from Austro-fascism and its institutions was *de facto* placing himself outside the church.

Yet, by giving its backing to a regime that was closer to Mussolini's Italian fascism than to Hitler's National Socialism, the Church was merely cutting its losses. It agreed, without any serious pangs of conscience, to back the scrapping of democracy, but at the same time it opposed the Austrian supporters of the Hitler regime which came to power in Berlin on January 1, 1933. The Nazis constituted a significant sector of Austrian political spectrum, and their influence was translated into important gains in the 1932 regional elections. The Nazis won 17% of the votes in Vienna, 29% in Salzburg, and 14% in Lower Austria, where the Waldheim family lived. The time had thus come for dramatic choices for the Austrian Catholics. They must either wholeheartedly support Chancellor Dollfuss's regime, or they must decide that an accommodation was desirable with the rising force of National Socialism, which, although nominally banned in Austria, was still very active.

After the assassination of Dollfuss on July 25, 1934, the National Socialists attempted a coup and the rift deepened between the anti-Nazi Catholics and those who were in favor of an alliance with Hitler's Austrian supporters. The Austrian Nazis had important support in the universities and in intellectual circles, as well as in influential magazines such as *Schoñerer Zukunft* (Brighter Future), which were to prepare the Catholic intelligentsia to enthusiastically welcome the Anschluss. Despite the rather confused efforts of Christian Socialist leaders such as Deputy Mayor of Vienna, Ernst Kartl Winter, to establish a sacred union against the rise of National Socialism, the rallying to Hitler seemed irresistable. National Socialism had already won the hearts of almost the whole of the country's Protestant minority, who had always been more pan-Germanic in sentiment than the Catholic majority. All that remained was for it to win over a sizeable proportion of Catholic opinion, and the road to Vienna would be wide open. The zenith of this Nazi conquest of the Austrian Catholic church came with the solemn declaration of the Austrian bishops published on March 18, 1938, one week after German troops had marched into the country. "From the depths of their conviction and completely of their own free will, the undersigned bishops of the provinces of Austria hereby declare concerning the great historical events which have just taken place in German Austria: we note with joy the results gained by the National Socialist movement in the field of economic and ethnic (*völkisch*) reconstruction for the German Reich and its people, especially the underprivileged classes. We are also convinced that thanks to the action of the National Socialist movement, the danger of destructive and atheistic bolshevism can be removed. The bishops append to this action their most sincere wishes for a victory and urge the believers work toward this end." This solemn declaration was accompanied by a handwritten letter from Cardinal Innitzer ending with the greeting, *"Heil Hitler!"*

The Tradition of Anti-Semitism

Austria between the wars was also the European country which displayed the most varied range of anti-Semites and the most diverse forms of anti-Semitism. It was during his stay in Vienna at the beginning of the century that Adolf Hitler saw the light which enabled him to found his theory and embark on his political career. The Jews were held responsible for everything that was bad. As soon as one left the Social Democratic and liberal circles of the capital city, one could not help encountering one or other of the shades of anti-Semitism. In the countryside, the ritual murder legend was still current, according to which Jews needed Christian blood to make their unleavened bread for Passover. Educated circles and the universities were dominated by the racism of Georg von Schönerer, a theoretician and anti-Semitic politician of the late nineteenth century whose theories were the precursors of Hitler's own.

The mildest form of this state of mind was to be found in the large masses influenced by the Church and the Christian Social party. As Dirk van Arkel has written in an important study of Austrian anti-Semitism[8], "most of the current stereotypes in anti-Jewish sentiment in Austria can already be found in newspapers such as *Die Weckstimme für das katholische Volk* (Catholic People's Reveille) and other conservative and right-wing Catholic publications published between 1871 and 1873. Devout Catholics, angered by the spread of anticlericalism and the secularization of government, were among the first to mount a frontal attack against the Jews. Take, for instance, the case of Josef Scheicher, a priest who in the *Wiener Kirchenzeitung* (Vienna Church Newspaper) launched the idea that 'pork-eating Jews', i.e. assimilated Jews, were the most dangerous kind and that the press was dominated by 'Judaised Christians'."

However, the man who most profoundly influenced public opinion in this area was undoubtedly Karl Lueger, founder of the Christian Social Party and Mayor of Vienna at the turn of the century. He represented the populist form of anti-Semitism, the type which one could experience in the middle classes who had been the victims of the economic crisis caused by modernization, and who blamed Jewish financiers for their misfortunes. This brilliant demagogue, a self-confessed cynic, having gained the highest of honors, declared one day, "Anti-Semitism is a sport for the populace which no longer serves a purpose when one has reached the top." The abolition of the property ownership qualification for the right to vote in 1882 permitted the development of an anti-Semitism for electoral purposes which Lueger exploited to the full to strengthen his position. This did not prevent him from assiduously cultivating some of the most prominent Jews in Vienna at the time, and even attending services at the Great Synagogue, wearing a skull-cap. "I decide who is a Jew!" This phrase often attributed to Hermann Goering is in fact Lueger's, in answer to some of his supporters who reproached him for making compromises.

"I learned anti-Semitism from Lueger in Vienna", writes Hitler in *Mein Kampf*. Soon the student would outstrip the teacher, but as soon as he entered Veinna, he was to find willing ears who discovered in the Führer the same tones they had heard from the old *Bürgermeister* who had done so much for the city.... Today, part of the Ring, the great avenue which encircles the center of Vienna, still bears the name of

Karl Lueger. No voice within the Roman Catholic camp has ever been heard to condemn the anti-Semitism of the first leaders of the Christian Social Party. The episcopate, which was concerned above all to retain the advantages won during the monarchy, and countering the secular and liberal movement which was developing in society, quickly suppressed any reservations it might have had about the anti-Semitic excesses of the Christian nation. The anti-Semitic extremists among the clergy were never condemned, and when Pope Leo XIII gave his blessing to the Austrian Christian Social party, part of whose program he borrowed for his encyclical *Rerum Novarum*, this was accepted.

An Anti-Nazi Father

How did this psychological and political context influence the young Waldheim? The attitudes he has adopted throughout his life, the course of study he selected, his choice of friends, the ideological and conceptual context in which his formative years were spent all served to shape him into the man he is today. Some of the strong language he used in the heat of the 1986 electoral campaign is most revealing. When French journalist Claire Tréan asked him his opinion on the negative attitude which the world's press had adopted, he replied: "But the international press is dominated by the World Jewish Congress. It's well known!"[9]

However, the young Kurt Waldheim could have chosen to resist Nazism, as did quite a number of his Christian compatriots and some of his fellow students in Tulln,[10] having realized that the values extolled by National Socialism were hardly those of his childhood and adolescence. He could at least have imitated his father by choosing internal exile and the silence which, as will be seen later, followed his arrest and his forced early retirement. Yet this was not to be the case.

In an observant and traditionalist Catholic family like Walter Waldheim's, the only member entitled to carry the banner of family beliefs was the father. Right up until his departure for military service in 1936, and particularly until he began his studies in Vienna in 1937, Kurt seems to have been a party to the options defended by Walter Waldheim. These were an unconditional attachment to the corporate Christian state of Chancellor Dollfuss and his successor, Kurt von Schuschnigg.

There are various facts to support this hypothesis, foremost of which is the political atmosphere then prevalent in Tulln. Just before they were banned, the percentage of votes cast for the Nazis in the Tulln district was actually lower than the national average. Under the authority of prominent local Catholics who were less obsessed by the Red peril, in any case little in evidence here, than were their opposite numbers in other regions, the right-wingers of Tulln were less attracted than others by the lure of National Socialism, which had never gained a deep hold on the peasantry, in either Germany or Austria.

Moreover, all the descriptions currently available of Walter Waldheim's personality show him to be a man dedicated to order, duty, and tradition. To him, the Nazis represented a certain form of chaos, different in nature but comparable in intensity to that which might be created by the Reds. Above all, he was concerned with his children's future. His second son, Walter, had already chosen to be a teacher like his father, and his studies were going very well. Kurt, the eldest, more secretive and less expansive, did not seem to have chosen his vocation by the time he left the *Klosterneuberg* high school from which he graduated with brilliant examination results in June 1936. Despite his lack of ability in math, his excellent grades in Latin and modern languages had ensured his success. The third child, Gerlinde, had long ago chosen her vocation. She wanted to be a doctor and would do anything to achieve her ambition. For these family goals to be realized, it was important that there should be no fundamental changes in their situation, so that order could prevail within the family, as well as outside it.

The choice of Walter Waldheim, the paterfamilias, not to become a Nazi, whatever his motives for doing so, was thus very real. It was translated into a short incarceration in the aftermath of the *Anschluss* and by an administrative posting nearly 40 miles away from Tulln, to Baden-bei-Wien. These sanctions were the result of a denunciatiation by the Tulln Nazis, who had a fight with young Kurt while he was distributing anti-Nazi tracts in favor of Chancellor Schuschnigg in the town, on the eve of the entry of German troops into Austria. Between 1938 and 1945, Walter Waldheim did not distinguish himself by taking any political stance. Sent into retirement, he was constrained to exile himself to Baden-bei-Wien. Can Kurt Waldheim plead his father's anti-Nazi attitude in order to reject the accusations made against himself?

Questioned in November, 1980 by Congressman Stephen J. Solarz about his eventual ties with Nazi movements Kurt Waldheim replied, "Above all, I would like to say that I was never associated in any way with the Nazi youth movement. On the contrary, my whole family was well-known for being actively anti-Nazi before the Anschluss, and we made no secret of our family convictions afterwards. It is true that my father was arrested after the Anschluss and that our family were forced to move due to constant harrassment by the Nazi authorities."

SA Cavalry Troop 5/90

KURT Waldheim's membership in three Nazi organizations is proved in a document from the archives of the Reich Ministry of Justice which was published in March, 1986 by the Austrian magazine *Profil*. What was published was a questionnaire produced in 1940 for appointing judges. In the section headed "Political Affiliation", one can read, "5/90 SA Cavalry Troop, SA Member since November 18, 1938, Member of the National Socialist Student Federation since April 1, 1938."

When confronted with this document, which clearly contradicts all his previous statements, Kurt Waldheim practised his elastic defense, adapting himself to whatever the circumstances under which he is asked to justify himself. "This is a monstrous lie, I have never been a member of a Nazi organization. This whole affair is a machination concocted for electoral purposes," he said to the Austrian newspaper *Kronenzeitung* on February 3, 1986. However, since he was unable to deny that he had been a member of the SA Cavalry troop, having admitted as much in the questionnaire which he had completed for his reintegration into the Austrian Ministry of Justice in 1945, he stated a month later: "This was just a sporting activity. It had nothing to do with the Party."

This sports argument, questionable in itself, could not be applied to the other organizations, the SA and the Nazi students. He gave two contradictory explanations. The first one is that the form must have been completed by his friends while he was at the front, who thought they were doing the right thing and protecting him by claiming that he belonged to Nazi organizations (from an interview with Associated Press on March 9, 1986). The second explanation is that his membership of these organizations was purely a formality and designed to keep up appearances, a protection to allow him to continue to study at university. "If I wanted to complete my studies, I needed some protection ... the [Nazi] students' association was nothing, it was quite harmless, it was an association which was joined mostly by people who wanted to carry on studying without getting into trouble." (*International Herald Tribune*, March 5, 1986). Finally, in his memorandum to the Austrian President Rudolf Kirchschläger, dated April 12, 1986, Waldheim repeated his first argument, "Despite the evidence in the documentation, I have never been a member of the NSDAP, nor of the Brownshirts (SA), nor of the Association of Nazi Students...."

Kurt Waldheim's defense is reminiscent of the old Jewish joke about the pot. An old Jew goes and asks his neighbor to return the pot he lent him. "You have come here for nothing," the neighbor replies. "I'll give you three reasons. First of all, you never lent me a pot. Second, it had a hole in it. Third, I gave it back to you long ago." However, the excuses developed by Kurt Waldheim to deny or minimize his membership in Nazi movements deserve to be studied closely because if such membership had been proved from 1945 onward, it might, at least for a time, have prevented him from holding public office, and might have had a considerable effect on his subsequent career.

If one is to believe him, the statements contained in the file and made in his name might have been communicated in his absence by well-intentioned friends. Apart from the fact that none of these friends has ever appeared to confirm what the Austrian President said, it should be noted that this file was compiled in spring, 1940 on the basis of a questionnaire that Kurt Waldheim had completed on April 24, 1940 to offer himself as a candidate for a judgeship. Under the rules then in force, the questionnaire would have had to be completed in person and under oath.

The document can now be seen in the archives of the Vienna Superior Court (*Oberlandesgericht Wien*). Under the heading concerned with membership of the National Socialist Party, the NSDAP, it states, "Not yet possible, since at present serving in the military." This is clearly a reply made in person. In any case, the theory that this document was completed in Kurt Waldheim's absence while he was serving in France in the German army does not hold water because the regimental leave records show that he was on leave from April 1 through October 15, 1940.

So from 1945 onward, Kurt Waldheim decided to lie by merely admitting to membership of the SA Cavalry. The reason is simple. When the Austrian administration had to be de-Nazified, those concerned were classified by virtue of their degree of involvement with the Nazi Party. Under the criteria established by the University of Vienna De-Nazification Commissions, which were composed of representatives of the three political parties permitted by the Allies (People's Party, Socialists, Communists), those who had only belonged to one Nazi mass movement were pardoned. However, those who had belonged to several organizations, thus displaying a degree of activity which exceeded the mere keeping up of appearances were penalized. Kurt Waldheim had three memberships; he had belonged to the SA Cavalry, the SA, and the Nazi student organization, so he had two too many.

A Brownshirt in 1938

W<small>HAT</small> is he hiding? What were the tangible realities beneath these memberships, if one sets aside the equestrian activities of the 5/90 SA Cavalry Troop? Kurt Waldheim's own version is unenlightening, and with good reason. However, the authors have obtained a photograph showing him in Nazi student uniform on guard on the Heldenplatz in Vienna, during a mass meeting organized by Gauleiter Bürckel shortly after the Anschluss on May 1, 1938. Confronted with this photograph, Kurt Waldheim simply said that the person in the photo must be his double.

The date on which he joined the SA Storm Troopers, better known as the Brownshirts, November 18, 1938, could exonerate him from having participated in the famous Crystal Night on November ninth, during which the full force of violence was unleashed against the Jews in the Reich and in Vienna. However, it should be noted that a six-month apprenticeship had to be served between an application to join the SA and full membership of the Brownshirts. During this period, the candidate would have to prove himself particularly enthusiastic.

The evidence of one of Kurt Waldheim's contemporaries, Albert Massiczek, who was also a university student, gives some idea of the duties of a student member of a National Socialist organization during the early days after the Anschluss.[11] Massiczek, who had already belonged to the illegal SS organization before the annexation, had begun to have his doubts about the Nazi cause immediately following German entry into the country. He managed to get himself discharged from the SS on the excuse that it was incompatible with the pursuit of his studies. This noticeable withdrawal from active service was interrupted by a telephone call in the night of November 9, 1938. Massiczek also notes that military exercises and the guarding of various buildings belonging to the Party were daily duties for Nazi students.

SA activity in the streets of Vienna intensified between March 1938 and September 1939, the date of the declaration of war, which obliged quite a number of the stormtroopers to don a different uniform, that of the Wehrmacht. The brutal treatment inflicted on the Jews and opponents of Nazism was far worse in Vienna than anywhere else. Under the iron rule of the men in brown, not a day passed without one being able to witness scenes of violence and humiliation in one district or another.

George Clare, an Austrian Jew and an eyewitness who left Vienna after the Anschluss, describes these moments as follows: "The whole city behaved like an aroused woman, vibrating, writhing, moaning and sighing lustfully for orgasm and release." This is not purple writing. It is an exact description of what Vienna was and felt like on Monday, March 14, 1938, as Hitler entered. And as the Führer's motorcade passed through the streets of the old Hapsburg city, lined by hundreds of thousands waving, jubilant Viennese, its church bells rang out their own obscene jubilation.

"That was what Vienna was like on that day. I know, I was there. But I also know that there were many thousands, not only Jews, who stayed away behind tightly-closed windows in order not to hear the frenzy of the streets. Those were the men and women who had genuine convictions. Social-Democrats, Legitimists, true Catholics, Christian-Socialists, who put patriotism before opportunism, as well as people who were neither this or not that but just honest human beings. What they felt during those hours, sadness shame and defiance,and a resolve to stand together as Austrians one day, was in due course to bridge the chasms that had divided them for so long and, eventually, provide the moral foundations on which the Second Republic was built.

"The Austrian Catholic Adolf Hitler, standing upright in his Mercedes car, his right hand raised in the Nazi salute, beheld the crowds of Austrian Catholics welcoming him to their city, a city that once took no notice of him. He never forgave Vienna this original slight. He resolved that not his Austrian, but his German paladins would be the future masters here."[12]

Another document deserves to be quoted at length for its revelations about daily life in Vienna in 1938. In previous years, Kurt Waldheim had been able to calmly explain that he was never aware of the persecutions suffered by the Jews. A similar amnesia is evident in a city which even now, in 1987, has still not erected the smallest monument or commemorative plaque to the memory of the 60,000 or so Viennese Jews exterminated by Nazism. Yet here is what a simple witness could see while walking down the Taborstrasse, in the Jewish quarter of Vienna, a few days after the Anschluss.[13] This story was published in 1939 in London.

What Waldheim Must Have Known

"Outside a big Jewish store stood a long string of lorries into which storm-troopers were pitching all kinds of millinery goods as they took them from the shop. Police stood by to see that they were not interfered with in the work of plunder and moved on the curious. There was nothing remarkable in this — it was just one incident which I happened to see myself among thousands. This was private plunder — for some reason considered more reprehensible than the systematic plundering the Nazi organization as such which stole Jewish businesses, some of which had been built up slowly for generations, and ruined some of them in a few months. Amidst all the horrors to which Austrian Jews, Austrian patriots and Austrian democrats — in fact, all non- Nazis — have been exposed ever since March 11th, the loss of every remedy against theft and plunder is the least. After a few days I do not think I heard any complaints or anxieties expressed by Jews on this score; it was just accepted as inevitable.

"Much more terrible was the acceptance of suicide as a perfectly normal and natural incident by every Jewish household. It is quite impossible to convey to anyone outside Austria in how matter-of-fact a way the Jews of Austria today refer to this way out of their agony. When I say one's Jewish friends spoke to one of their intention to commit suicide with no more emotion than they had formerly talked of making an hour's journey by train, I cannot expect to be believed. Nevertheless, the fact must be recorded. It is not your fault that you cannot believe me, because it is impossible for you to conceive of the diseased and degenerate mentality which lies behind the pathological Anti-Semitism of the Nazis. Therefore it is impossible for you to imagine what it means for one-sixth of the population of Vienna to be made pariahs overnight, deprived of all civil rights, including the right to retain property large or small, the right to be employed or to give employment, to exercise a profession, to enter restaurants, cafés, bathing beaches, baths or public parks, to be faced daily and hourly, without hope of relief, with the foulest insults which ingenious and vicious minds can devise, to be liable always to turned overnight out of house and home, and at any hour or every day and every night to arrest without the pretence of a charge or hope of a definite sentence, however heavy—and with all this to find every country in the world selfishly closing its frontiers to you when, after being plundered of your last farthing, you seek to escape. For most of the non-Jewish victims of the Nazis, many of whom are now sharing the punishment of the Jews, there is a hope that one day the nightmare may pass. For the Jews there is none while the Nazis rule.

"It is no fault of yours, but your very good fortune, that you cannot believe that one after another families are being turned out of their houses and herded into a ghetto merely because they are not of undiluted Teutonic blood, that in their thousands men and women are still being arrested, held in crowded cells for months without the suggestion of any guilt or charge, and when called upon to sign a promise to leave the country forthwith or go to Dachau—knowing full well that there is not a country they can enter. You cannot believe the stories you read in your newspapers of Jewish families, after living for generations in Burgenland villages, being taken out to an island breakwater—children, old men and women, cripples of eighty and more, and very sick persons—and abandoned in the midst of a raging storm in the Danube, whose swirling, muddy brown waters lap their feet. It cannot make any real impression on your consciousness as things which are really happening daily and hourly ... to hear that these peasant or shopkeeping families were rescued, refused anywhere an asylum, and are to this day huddled together on an ancient vessel in mid-stream—as are others in filthy, desolate Alpine huts in a triangle of No-Man's-Land between three countries and in the dank fields of Bohemia outside the new German frontiers.... Women, whose husbands had been arrested a week before without any charge, receive a small parcel from the Viennese postman with the curt intimation—'To pay, 150 Marks, for the cremation of your husband—ashes enclosed from Dachau.' The usual intimation is just a printed slip, a copy of which lies before me: 'The relatives of _____ are informed herewith that he died today at Dachau Concentration Camp. (*Signed*) STAPO HEADQUARTERS.' A professional man came with ashen face and loose, quivering lips to the journalist he had often attended and babbling out: 'Hide my son, hide him—last week they took my cousin's boy to Dachau and sent back the ashes in an urn four days later.' ... You have never seen Nazis gloating over the daily suicide lists, you have not looked into the indescribably bestial pages of Julius Streicher's *Der Stürmer*, or seen the slavering mouth of this scarlet-faced, bald-headed vulture beside whom I have more than once drunk beer in Munich and read his headlines above the stories of suicides in Vienna: 'Recommended as an Example to Others....'

"Some of the horrors I saw at very close quarters. Hurrying down the stairs of my flat to hear Hitler make his first speech on his arrival in Vienna, I was delayed by men carrying out the bodies of a young Jewish doctor and his mother, who had lived, quiet, decent and hard-working neighbours for years, two floors below. The man had been dismissed from his hospital overnight without a hope of ever being allowed to earn another penny. Nazis had forced their way into his flat and thrust a great Swastika banner out of his window. Being a doctor, escape was easier for him and his mother than for most; they had found it through a hypodermic syringe. The

S.S. guards in the basement premises, who had replaced
Schuschnigg's Sturmkorps, stood around grinning their satisfaction as the bodies came out. From my window I could
watch for many days how they would arrest Jewish passers-
by—generally doctors, lawyers or merchants, for they preferred
their victims to belong to the better educated classes—and
force them to scrub, polish and beat carpets in the flat where
the tragedy had taken place, insisting the while that the non-
Jewish maid should sit at ease in a chair and look on. My
street, the Hapsburgergasse, was made a park for stolen Jewish
cars, on which the S.S. had painted their dreaded insignia. I
could not enter or leave my house all the time I was in Vienna
without having to witness the degrading spectacle of Jewish
men of all social ranks and ages and Jewish ladies and young
girls collected at random on the streeets—every non-Jew wore
the swastika so they were easily recognized—doing press-gang
labour, washing the cars stolen from their co-racials.

"Mine proved a good center, too, for watching the favorite
amusement of the Nazi mobs during many long weeks of
forcing Jewish men and women to go down on hands and
knees and scrub the pavements with acid preparations which
bit into the skin, obliging them to go straight to hospital for
treatment. Under Dollfuss and Schuschnigg, in a certain number
of cases where Nazis were caught painting up the forbidden
Swastika, they were made by the police to paint them over
with black paint or to sweep up with a broom the paper
Swastikas they scattered in the streets—a mild and appropriate
measure which can hardly even be considered punishment.
Apologists for the Nazis abroad have tried to draw a parallel
between this and the pavement-washing inflicted on the Jews.
The parallel is non-existent. Whereas the Nazis were taken in
the early hours of the morning, before many people were about,
to remove the illegal propaganda which in defiance of the law
they had themselves spread overnight, the Jews were now taken
to the most-frequented streets at the hour when their humiliation would be greatest, and forced to remove all traces of the
absolutely legal, electoral propaganda of the previous Government, with the preparation of which they had had nothing to

do. As soon as Dr. Schuschnigg announced the plebiscite, the members of his youth organization, as I saw myself, painted on the pavements, on Dr. Schuschnigg's instructions, the 'Dollfuss Cross', or stencilled on walls the portrait of Schuschnigg. Now, day after day, Nazi storm-troopers, surrounded by jostling, jeering and laughing mobs of 'golden Viennese hearts', dragged Jews from shops, offices and homes, men and women, put scrubbing brushes in their hands, splashed them well with acid, and made them go down on their knees and scrub away for hours at the hopeless task of removing Schuschnigg propaganda. All this I could watch from my office window overlooking the Graben. (Where there was none available, I have seen Nazis painting it for the Jews to remove.) From time to time a roar of delight from the crowds would announce that the storm-troopers, saying mockingly, "Now you want more water", had sluiced their victim from a bucket of filthy water.

"The first 'cleaning squad' I saw was at the Praterstern in the Jewish quarter. It was employed on trying to wash off the stencilled portrait of Schuschnigg from the pediment of a statue. Through the delighted crowds storm-troopers dragged an aged Jewish working-man and his wife. With tears rolling silently down her cheeks, looking straight ahead and through her tormentors, the woman held her old husband's arm, and I could see her trying to pat his hand.

"'Work for the Jews at last, work for the Jews!' the mob howled. 'We thank our Führer for finding work for the Jews.'"

Waldheim-Zelig

In a very popular film he made in 1984, Woody Allen created a character called Zelig who would immediately take on the coloration of the circles in which he happened to be moving at the time. When he was with fat people he became obese, when he was with intellectuals he was neurotic, and he was even portrayed at a Nazi party rally at Nuremburg wearing an SA uniform and waving to friends. Kurt Waldheim has shown, throughout his life, an uncommon propensity for these chameleon-like mutations. He has a remarkable ability to sense a change in the political climate and to back the right horse at the right moment. Not everyone has been capable, as he was, of simultaneously becoming an opponent of Nazism in his own home town of Tulln and being an active member of the National Socialist organizations in Vienna. This is what appears to have been the true course of his life during the period between the end of his high school studies and the time when he joined the army in August 1939. Before he graduated from high school in 1936, Kurt Waldheim was entirely under his family's thumb, that is, opposed to the illegal Nazi party which wanted to accelerate the union between Austria and the Reich. One of his classmates, Josef Tasler, describes Waldheim the high school student in these terms: "He was pleasant, kind and quiet." Tasler founded the *Comagenia* fraternity at the Klosterneuberg high school. It was a high-school version of the *Burschenschaften*, those German student fraternities which were basically preoccupied with drinking sessions and the organization of duels from which the future German elite received those famous scars so admired by young girls of good family. The *Burschenschaften* fraternities were for the most part ardent propagandists of Nazi ideas. But at the time, Kurt Waldheim did not have a leadership mentality; he was simply a bodyguard of the fraternity leader.

The turning point in the relationship between Kurt Waldheim and his family came when he graduated from high school and decided to volunteer for military service for a year, to join an officers' training course. This was a higher education course for degree holders; most of the cadets were young men from bourgeois or aristocratic families. The latter, being volunteers, could choose the branch of the service in which they preferred to serve. Kurt Waldheim chose the dragoon regiment stationed at Stockerau, located on the left bank of the Danube between Tulln and Vienna, because it was near the family home.

This cavalry regiment, most of whose officers were scions of ancient noble households, was still strongly impregnated with the values of the old Empire. Kurt Waldheim, son of a minor official and grandson of a blacksmith, was a little lost in an atmosphere dominated by blueblood. He had never done any horseback riding and his sporting activities had been limited to canoeing along the backwaters of the Danube just behind his hometown. It was here that he gained a love of horsemanship which never left him. It was also here that he made the decision to become a diplomat and, despite his provincial awkwardness and plebian background, to enter a profession in which an aristocratic pedigree was the greatest advantage.

As soon as he had completed his military service in October, 1937, Kurt Waldheim registered simultaneously at the Faculty of Law in Vienna and the Consular Academy in the *Boltzmanngasse,* the breeding-ground of the Empire's diplomats, and later those of the Republic. As a student at the establishment he appeared to be at a disadvantage. His family were unable to bear the cost of his living in the capital—there were still two other children to care for—so Kurt Waldheim made the 25-mile train trip each day between Tulln and Vienna. Later, when his father was fired by the Nazis and the family moved to Baden-bei-Wien, the journey became shorter.

From the beginning, Kurt Waldheim proved to be an extraordinarily diligent student, as shown by his first semester's grades. One can feel that he was motivated by the desire to succeed despite all the difficulties inherent in his situation. While at home in the evening, he remained a worthy scion of the Waldheim family, impervious to the pressures exerted by the local Nazis, in Vienna he fell under the influence of teachers and fellow students who were converted to the cause of Hitler. As Alfred Massiczek remarks, "Before and after the Anschluss, the University of Vienna proved to be an especially fertile ground for Nazi recruitment and indoctrination."

When de-Nazification was carried out in 1945, although it was done with a certain laxity and only affected those professors whose compromises with the regime were indisputable, only ten lecturers out of the 34 members of the Law Faculty in which Kurt Waldheim studied were allowed to remain in their posts. Most of those who were removed were reinstated shortly afterwards under the 1948 amnesty laws, thus nullifying any effect that de-Nazification might have had.

However, one must differentiate between the Law Faculty, which even before the Anschluss was dominated by members of the still-illegal Nazi party, and the Consular Academy, where the dominant tendency was rather Catholic-conservative, and where the Nazi elements only surfaced after the annexation. Despite this, it was very far from being a center of resistance and the student body, most of whom intended to enter the diplomatic service of the Second Republic tried, more or less successfully, to reshape their traditionalist Pan-Germanic Catholic ideology to the requirements of the new masters. Until the significant March 13, 1938, the day of the Anschluss, Kurt Waldheim was a serious, conformist student in Vienna, who took no active part in politics. However, in Tulln, he was distributing anti-Nazi tracts in favor of Chancellor Schuschnigg. He needed only a few weeks to adapt to the new circumstances and enter the ranks of the defenders of the Nazi regime. On April 1, 1938, less than two weeks after Adolf Hitler's famous speech in the Heldenplatz in Vienna, he joined the Nazi students' union.

The Director of the Consular Academy, Friedrich Hlavac von Rechtwall, then sent on attachment a sort of political commissar, one Lambert Haibock, who had been active in the clandestine Nazi party. A few years later, Haibock would be expelled from the Nazi party on the grounds that he was a practicing Roman Catholic. While still a member of the Nazi Party, Lambert Haibock took the hard-working and deserving student Kurt Waldheim under his wing, seeing in him the type of new man which the Greater Reich's diplomatic corps needed. In fact, the Nazis were wary of the sons of the nobility, whose Hapsburg nostalgia did not fit the Hitler style.

When Kurt Waldheim applied for a scholarship to study in Italy, Haibock wrote him a letter of recommendation: "He incorporates in the best way the type of student of our time and of our country." This recommendation could not be applied, because war was soon declared and Kurt Waldheim was drafted.

While he was studying at the Law Faculty in Vienna, Kurt Waldheim also met the woman who was to become his wife, Elisabeth Ritschel. Four years younger, she is the daughter of an infantry officer. As a member of the NSDAP, the Nazi Party, since 1938, Elisabeth was very involved in the Nazi movement, even to the point of having left the Catholic church in order to adhere more closely to the Führer's ideology. She rejoined the church when she married Kurt Waldheim in 1944. However, according to her fellow students, this brown-haired girl with the steel-blue eyes, who was very proud of her father's military bearing, remained a loyal Nazi to the end. One of her classmates recalls, "She told me in January, 1945 that Kurt was in Vienna and that one had to hold on until the Reich's final victory." The combined influence of his teachers and his fiancée gradually detached Kurt Waldheim from the family ideology. They turned the anti-Nazi of Tulln into a zealous fellow-traveler down Hitler's road in every way, and a modest but essential cog in the Nazi war and terror machine.

A Pan-Germanic Thesis

ALTHOUGH accepted in 1944, Kurt Waldheim's doctoral thesis, "The Concept of Reich According to Konstantin
Frantz" (*Die Reichsidee bei Konstantin Frantz*) is part of
the ideological continuity of his student period. He was in-
spired to choose this subject by a professor of international
law, Alfred Verdross-Drossberg, who represented the Catholic
Pan-Germanic trend in the University of Vienna. Verdross-
Drossberg presented the keynote paper on the theme, "Christ
and the West" at the famous Congress of Austrian Catholics
in September 1933, during which the leaders of the Catholic
community aligned themselves almost unconditionally behind
the Hitler's concept of the "Greater Reich". (Hitler had just
come to power in Berlin.)

Alfred Verdross-Drossberg's thesis was that the concept
of the Reich should be given a theological justification by
assimilating it into the mystical body of Jesus, a privilege
formerly reserved for the church itself, and which hitherto
had never been applied to any earthly nation. This alliance
of the supports of the mystic Reich and the established Nazi
ideologues, of whom the best known is Alfred Rosenberg,
lasted only for a while and only as long as the pagan element
was not yet dominant in Hitlerite mythology when relations
between Nazis and Catholics began to deteriorate. At that
time, most of the Hitlerite Catholics broke away from Nazism,
some of them joined the resistance and others maintained a
deceitful silence.

However, at the time Kurt Waldheim chose his thesis,
just before he left to serve in the Wehrmacht, the break had
not yet occurred, and this choice is yet another proof of his
consummate adaptation to the dominant ideology. Other
students, less careful to keep on good terms with the Nazis,
devoted themselves to more neutral researches and some of

those who had placed themselves at the service of National Socialist knowledge in the euphoria of the Anschluss, ostentatiously changed their theses. This is what happened to Alfred Massiczek, for instance, who abandoned the subject of his research into "German Colonization in Eastern Europe" to work on Jansenism. But Kurt Waldheim devoted most of his army furloughs and the recreation time he got after his activities at the Heeresgruppe E command post to work on "The Concept of Reich According to Konstantin Frantz". In 1944, the fruits of his labors were translated into a 94-page memorandum, typed by his devoted fiancée, Elisabeth Ritschel, who was also his ideological mentor.

By strictly academic standards, this work is extremely mediocre. Basically, it consists of close paraphrases of the writings of Konstantin Franz, the student frequently omitting the quotation marks when he recopied whole passages by this author. Today, this piece of work would not even merit a master's degree. It could be claimed that the fact that the author was serving in the military and that he was working under certain unusual conditions swayed the jury in his favor and won him his doctorate with the grade of "good".

The Conservative Prussian statesman Konstantin Frantz (1817–1891), to whom Kurt Waldheim devoted his thesis, was one of Bismarck's collaborators. However, he deserted Bismarck when the "Iron Chancellor" opted for the founding of a German Reich under the rule of Prussia and the Hohenzollerns, excluding Austria and the Hapsburgs. Konstantin Frantz then devoted himself to promoting the idea of a Greater German Reich, in opposition to the Smaller Germany proposed by Bismarck. For Frantz, a Reich had to be created which would transcend societies and individual differences, one which would become the central element in a confederation of western and central Europe. His prime objective was to contain Russia, an Asiatic power "which must be pushed back not only to beyond the Danube but even beyond the Dniester." This overview involved submitting all the other nations to the concept of a Reich; pursuing the colonization and assimilation of the Slav populations of Poland and the Balkans; integrating those Germanic nations which had never previously been a part of it—the Dutch, Flemish, and Swiss—into the Reich; and making it clear to the non-Germanic powers, France, Spain, and Italy, that they had no business meddling in central Europe and that their destiny should lead them to look further afield toward the Levant and Africa.

2

The Hidden Years

We shall fight to the end
Until the devil receives his punishment
We shall show the world that it can have faith
In us, the youths aged less than twenty-two.
                    Song of the Yugoslav partisans

"In 1936, I served for a year as a volunteer in an Austrian cavalry regiment before entering university. Like many Austrians in my position, I was entered by the Nazi authorities on their rolls at the beginning of the war and I could not escape the draft. I was assigned to the 45th Aufklärung-Abteilung (A-A 45) of the Wehrmacht, a reconnaissance unit in whose mounted section I served. In no way did I have any contact with units involved in extermination. I myself was injured on the Russian front and classified unfit for service, which enabled me to resume my studies at the University of Vienna and obtain my degree in 1944." Of all the versions given by Kurt Waldheim of his falsified and abbreviated biography, this is the most revealing. It dates from December 19, 1980, when Waldheim, who was then Secretary-General of the United Nations, was writing a personal letter to U.S. Congressman Stephen J. Solarz, concerning the darker rumors about his past.[14]

Kurt Waldheim had been enraged by those questions. Here was a man with a strong penchant for honors and very sure of his own worth. He was about to solicit a third mandate at the head of the United Nations: "I was urged from all sides to offer my services," he notes modestly in his autobiography.[15] In actual fact, his office was contested and he was afraid the critics might seize the occasion to attack his Achilles heel. The terms in which his letter are couched were thus weighed very carefully. He denies any contact with the extermination units, and refrains from indicating any historical or geographical context in which he might have been in a position to be in contact with them. Between mentioning his injury on the Russian front and the idyllic completion of his studies in Vienna, there is a gap of two years, during which he had ample opportunity for such encounters with the extermination units, i.e., during his service in the Balkans.

"I must apologize to all my friends in the United States and Austria for not having mentioned this period. If I have acted wrongly in this way, I am very sorry. I shall make honorable amends." On April 13, 1986, Kurt Waldheim beat his breast on American television (*CBS News*, *Sixty Minutes*). Yet, when he was questioned two months later by a French radio station on the day after his election victory (*Europe I*, 6/16/86), he offered a dual explanation for omitting these important years. He considered, he said, that this detail would not interest anyone, and anyway that his time in Yugoslavia and Greece had not been eventful. "It was wartime. I was a young man of 20, 22. War is war. The German army's enemy in the Balkans, was the partisans. It was the war, it was a military confrontation."

Turning the events which took place in the region between 1942 and 1945 into commonplace banalities is merely an attempt to lay the foundations for Waldheim's self-absolution. It betrays his profound conviction that the Wehrmacht behaved under those circumstances like any other army in mid-campaign. Yet the viciousness of the Nazi repression is known, from the Kozara to the deportation of the Jews of Salonika, and that is why Kurt Waldheim desperately sought to end the story of his military career with his time on the eastern front, in Soviet territory. That is because Kurt Waldheim's memory loss is on two levels. He has certainly forgotten a number of the details of his Balkan campaign, as the laborious attempts at an historical reconstruction in the presence of various journalists have shown. However, he could not possibly have forgotten this long posting to one of the major fronts of Nazi expansionism.

The Early Military Career

W<small>ALDHEIM</small> certainly did not end his career under the swastika flag on December 17, 1941, when he was designated wounded by a shell burst in the right thigh in Byelorussia and hospitalized in the *Reservelazarett* (military hospital) in Minsk.[17] Kurt Waldheim had previously served one year in the military (from September 1, 1936 to August 31, 1937) as a volunteer in the 1st Dragoon Regiment based at Stockerau. In summer 1938, the Anschluss had already wiped out the independent Austrian state and young Waldheim was drafted to the Wehrmacht camp at Crampnitz, near Berlin, to train as a commando. In October, he was sent with the 4th Squadron of the 11th Cavalry Regiment into Sudetenland to participate in the occupation of that region. One month later, on November 18, he officially joined the SA Cavalry (*Sturmabteilung*), Unit 5/90 whose headquarters were at 19 Schuettelstrasse in the 2nd District of Vienna.

After a short stay in the 11th Reserve Cavalry Regiment at Stockerau, *Unteroffizier* Waldheim (a rank equivalent to master sergeant) was drafted into a reconnaissance detachment (A-A 45) of the 45th Infantry Division at Homberg, which was to participate in the invasion of France. From January 4 through October 15, 1940, he took leave to continue his university studies and became a *Gerichts-Referendar* (apprentice lawyer at the Vienna Bar). In a questionnaire preserved at the Vienna Superior Court, dated April 24, the candidate replies as follows to the question concerning membership of the National Socialist Party. "Not yet possible, because on active military service." After rejoining his unit which had been fighting the French campaign since May 25, Kurt Waldheim was promoted to the rank of reserve lieutenant in December.

Waldheim was then sent to the Russian and Polish

frontier with the 45th Reconnaissance Battalion, under the command of the man who was to become the Cossack general, Hellmuth von Pannwitz. From April 6, 1941, he commanded the first section of the Cavalry Squadron of that battalion. His fighting zeal was hardly in doubt. He received the *Eisernen Kreuz* (Iron Cross, Second Class) on July 3, 1941 (after the fall of Brest-Litovsk) then, on August 18, he was awarded the *Kavallerie-Sturmabzeichen* (Assault cavalry, Second Class) medal; later, in March 1942, he was honored with the *Ostmedaille*, the Eastern Front Medal.[18] On October 8, he took command of a whole cavalry squadron.

His injury did not allow him to return to his beloved studies and the anonymity of civilian life, but brought him closer to home. On January 15, 1942 he was transferred to Military Hospital XXIII C in Vienna. He was classified fit for service on March 6 and returned to his former regiment, the 11th Cavalry in which he had served in Sudentenland in October 1938. But eight days later, on March 14, he was posted to the *Oberkommando Heeresgruppe E* (High Command of Group E) of the 12th Army Corps (AOK 12). The cavalry officer had avoided a posting to a fighting unit and, like thousands of very young men in the Wehrmacht, was drafted into staff duties in a sector of the army which, in conjunction with the *Kampfgruppe* (Combat Group) in western Bosnia, would play a decisive role in the progress of the war. At the time, the Wehrmacht had a serious manpower problem.

Total War Against the Yugoslav Partisans

SHORTLY after he arrived at his new posting, Waldheim was sent to Pljevlja (Yugoslavia) to serve as a liaison officer and interpreter at the headquarters of the *Kampfgruppe Bader*.[19] The mission of this unit, in close collaboration with the Italian Pusteria Division, was to eliminate pockets of Yugoslav partisans in the Sarajevo, Dubrovnik and Pljevlja region. In April 1941, Yugoslavia was divided into zones of influence between Germany, Italy, Bulgaria, Hungary and Albania. Two puppet states, Pavelić's Croatia and Nedić's Serbia, were established by the Nazis, but in practice the Germans were running the country. The 342nd German Division was withdrawn from France to serve as reinforcements in the fight against the partisans. On November 29, 1941 the resistance fighters led by Tito lost the "Uzice Republic" a territory they had protected against the Nazi advance.[20] Defeated in the battle of Pljevlja on December 1, they pulled back to the River Drina.

Kurt Waldheim's main task was to serve as *Dolmetscher* (interpreter) between the German and the Italian commands. He knew Italian, as well as French and English, and had begun to learn Serbo-Croat.[21] Even in his very specialized function, the violence of the fighting and brutality of the occupation could not have been unknown to him. On May 23, 1942, an official report concluded that the resistance movement in the German zone of eastern Bosnia has been destroyed by the Trio I and Foca campaigns of the Bader Combat Group. It was at this time that the Nazi authorities issued the reprisal ratios against the local population: "100 Serbs to be executed for every German killed, 50 Serbs for every German wounded."

From March 19 onward, the instructions of the commander-in-chief of the 12th Army were explicit: "The most minor case of rebellion, resistance, or concealment of arms must be treated immediately by the strongest deterrent methods. The troops must be trained to retaliate with maximum force in these circumstances. The more implacable and explicit the measures adopted henceforth, the less will be the need for them in the future. No sentimentality (*Keine*

Gefühlsduselei)! It is better to liquidate 50 suspects than have one soldier killed!"

In June, Lieutenant Waldheim was sent to the *Kampfgruppe Westbonien* where he was attached to headquarters. He was listed in 25th place out of 34 officers in the 12th army corps noted for their valor.[22] The west Bosnian Combat Group, based at Banja Luka (north of Pljevlja), consisted in part of the Bader Combat Group. Combat against the partisans had moved on the map of Yugoslavia, and now concentrated on attacking the resistance zone in the Kozara Mountains.

Under the command of General Friedrich von Stahl, 72,000 men (18,000 of them Croatians) prepared to fight one of the bitterest battles of World War II, on a territory of just over 30,000 square miles. In an interview with the Yugoslav daily *Vecernje Novosti* (April 2, 1986), Kurt Waldheim contradicted his previous statements by admitting that he had been in Pljevlja at that time. Thirteen days later, he told an Italian newspaper, *La Repubblica* that he was, indeed, based in Banja Luka but that he had spent most of his time gossiping and playing cards with Mussolini's General Esposito in a little café. His role would have been confined to liaison missions between the German command and the Italian troops, yet, in the opinion of all the historians, the Italians took no part in the Kozara offensive.

The outcome of that battle was crucial for the Third Reich. At the time, the position of the Yugoslav resistance fighters appeared to be desperate. "They had only a limited number of pressure points, the partisans grouped at the point where Montenegro and Bosnia-Herzegovina met, and a few combat units fighting in western Bosnia."[23] Kurt Waldheim would seek to minimize the significance of this event in retrospect, and especially the barbarism with which the civilian population had been crushed. In the Wehrmacht's balance sheet compiled on August 29, 1942, 4,735 "insurgents" were declared dead, as against 71 German soldiers, but the report says nothing about the number of reprisal victims, and makes no mention of the 68,000 peasants, most of them women and children, who were deported to concentration camp.[24] As far as Waldheim was concerned—he said so on Austrian Television on March 25, 1986—"There was no massacre in the Kozara Mountains, it is absurd to use this term, it was a tough battle, a cruel war." When the candidate for the presidency of Austria began to realize the deep psychological scar that this episode has left in the Yugoslav national conscience, one which still hurts today, he became more reticent. However, the fact is that if many Yugoslav journalists have decided to research the archives at whatever personal cost, it is precisely because Kurt Waldheim's participation in the battles of Kozara and Sutjeska seemed to them to constitute overwhelming evidence of his guilt. Iovan Kessar, a reporter on the Yugoslav newspaper *Vecernje Novosti* told us in Belgrade, "The Kozara reflected the whole cruelty of this war, the consequences of the partition of Yugoslavia, the free hand given to the Croatian fascists to settle old scores."

A Very Active Interpreter

On July 22, 1942, Lieutenant Waldheim received the medal of the Order of Zvonimir, an award from the Nazi-run puppet state of Croatia. It was to reward his heroic courage in battle against the rebels in spring and summer, 1942. In the apologia he made public on April 12, 1986, the recipient claimed that this medal was handed out to anyone and everyone, and that it had been awarded to him for exploits prior to his posting to Kozara, despite the fact that the official citation states exactly the opposite.

It is hard to see why a German officer stationed at

Pljevlja would be honored by the Croatian authorities, whose sphere of influence was much further to the west. Waldheim's name appears in third place on the list of 12 men drawn up by General Stahl on August 6, 1942 as an official notification that they received this medal. According to the most authoritative historian of the Fascist State of Croatia, Bogdan Kryszman, the Order of Zvonimir was not bestowed lightly. For him, the mere fact that Waldheim received and accepted it makes him unworthy to preside over the United Nations. It should be added that the decoration he won bore oak leaves, a special mark for acts of bravery under enemy fire.

Previously, Kurt Waldheim might merely have been a petty bureaucrat, a man without qualities in the heart of the formidable German war machine. He was, indeed, an extremely zealous official; shortly before he was granted four-and-a-half months leave to return to Vienna to finish his studies, he was promoted to *Oberleutnant*, First Lieutenant, on November 19, 1942. His superior during Operation Schwarz in 1943, Lieutenant-Colonel Bruno Willers, was to say of him that he was "an officer who did his duty, a discreet and reserved man." Another of his superiors, Herbert Warnstorff, hailed him as an executive officer "who did what was expected of him, that is, very satisfactory work."[25]

When Kurt Waldheim absented himself from the Balkan front, the conflict in the region was at a turning point. After having suffered serious setbacks, the 38 "proletarian" brigades active in Yugoslavia decided to organize all the partisan groups into the "Yugoslav National Liberation Army and Partisan Detachments" in November, 1942. This consisted of nine divisions (comprising between 3,000 and 4,000 men) and two army corps (of about 10,000 fighting men).[26] Tito authorized continuation of the guerilla war, despite this more orthodox restructuring of the armed resistance forces. "We must not fear encirclement, any more than we did at a time when we had fewer units available. Any loss of territory must be translated into the conquest of another territory, a bigger and more strategic one." In order to measure the scope of what was at stake, one must remember that on February 21, 1943, the BBC was claiming from London that, "The Yugoslav partisans represent the only organized military force fighting at present in Europe...."

Faced with this new formation, the Wehrmacht also reorganized itself. On January 1, 1943, the section of the 12th Army Corps to which Waldheim belonged—the rest having been sent to the Russian front—was reorganized into a military formation better adapted to combatting guerrilla warfare. This new section, Heeresgruppe E, had its headquarters at Arsakli, 3¾ miles from the center of Salonika in northern Greece. Hitler had established an overt link between the repression of Communist resistance in Greece and Yugoslavia and the offensive against the Soviet Union. "If the struggle against the guerrillas is not waged in the East and in the Balkans by the most radical means, it will very soon be impossible to find forces in sufficient number to eradicate this vermin.... This fight has nothing whatever to do with the rules of chivalry or the Geneva Convention."[27]

The hardening of the German line upset the equilibrium that had been established with Mussolini's occupation forces. The situation could be summarized as follows: "The occupying forces exploited disagreements between the nations which make up Yugoslavia, stirred up by middle-class leaders between the wars, in order to ignite a civil war between them. This is how the Ustashis came to commit the first massacres of the Serbs, with German permission, while the Catholic clergy forced the Serbian population of Croatia to convert to Catholicism. By taking over the wealthiest regions and the strategically im-portant means of communication, the Germans gained a controlling position. Italy won considerably less. The two allies tended to use the population of the occupied regions firstly in industrial labor, as well as for military production, to exploit Yugoslavia's natural resources according to their military requirements."[28]

The Italian army, which was much more psychologically vulnerable to the hostility of the local population, tended to yield, and the German high command decided more often than not to give up its collaboration. The translation talents of Kurt Waldheim were only required for delicate negotiations when he returned to the front on March 31, 1943, assigned to Group E headquarters.

Historical evidence is lacking to establish what Kurt Waldheim did during his first two months at General Alexander Loehr's headquarters. This gap is very worrying, because it coincides with the start of deportation operations against the Jews of Salonika. However, it is certain that Loehr, who was also Viennese, knew his subordinate well and would not have hesitated to assign important tasks to him. On May 22, 1943, as can be seen in a photograph, Waldheim was at the Podgorica Airport (now known as Titograd) in Montenegro. The Wehrmacht liaison group, formerly stationed at Tirana, moved here mainly to convince the Italian forces to join Operation Schwarz against the partisans.

The Austrian politician claims to have played no part whatever in this action, which involved 72,000 German soldiers and started on May 15. Yet this was the sole purpose of the meeting on May 22 in Podgorica, to which Colonel Hans Herbert Macholz had been sent by General Loehr in the company of Lieutenant Waldheim. He had to persuade the Italian General, Escola Roncaglia, to throw himself into battle without restraint. A weighty argument was found in the presence of the Waffen-SS General Arthur Phleps, Commander of the Prinz-Eugen SS Division whose expeditious methods even shocked Oberführer Werner Fromm after the extermination of the little Yugoslav village of Kosutica. Kurt Waldheim only remembered that differences of opinion emerged on that occasion between Roncaglia and Macholz. But the stake was very high. The Italians had to be forced to join in the repression to include women and children (so states a Wehrmacht order of the day dated December 16, 1942), together with men under the command of Phleps, himself a former officer in the Austrian imperial army.

At a time when during the space of one month more than 16 thousand people had been killed—mostly during blind reprisals—Kurt Waldheim features in army records as an *Ordonnanzoffizier,* a staff officer with special duties. Four decades later, he "no longer remembers anything."[29], but at the time his main task was to counter the demoralizing effects of partisan activities on the 14th Italian Army. Partisan demoralization tactics became more and more effective. A leaflet dated July 11, 1943 declares, "Italian brothers, come and join our Liberation Army, come and fight in our ranks! This is the decisive moment, all honest, patriotic and anti-Fascist men of whatever nationality must unite in the fight for freedom."

Kurt Waldheim's military career thus precisely followed the parameters of hostilities. At first he was assigned to ordinary interpreting duties, where the young officer found himself directly involved in operational missions before making an extremely effective contribution to the psychological work aimed at the Italian troops. He was neither a tribune nor an oracle, but he manifested this small sense of honor, this passion for mediocrity which Robert Musil, yet again diagnosed in his time as prevalent among Austrian bureaucrats, this calculating aloofness which would impress Italian troops who were at the prey of confusion and uncertainty.

In Salonika During the Deportations

IN early July, 1943—only two weeks after the official conclusion of Operation Schwarz, which is proof enough of how valuable his services were to General Loehr—Kurt Waldheim was appointed second in command (under another veteran of Operation Schwarz, Bruno Willers) of Group Ia, at Wehrmacht headquarters at the 11th Italian Army, based in Athens. It was an important job. Under rule 92 of the Staff Service Manual published in 1938, Group Ia was entrusted with all the operational missions and could make decisions on this basis in the absence of the operational commander and the chief of staff.

Evidently, Waldheim's prerogatives were limited to joint German-Italian operations. However, these operations were not merely routine. On August 7, 1943 for instance, Waldheim's office sent a secret message 959-43 (Ia) recommending on the order of the Führer, summary execution of bandits (partisans) captured in combat, and to send the suspects into *Sauckel* work camps in Germany. Under the Charter of the Nuremberg Tribunal these two types of action were classified as crimes against humanity and war crimes.

From July 9 through August 21, 1943, the Oberleutnant was also entrusted with maintaining the official war diary of the staff command (*Kriegstagebuch*). According to his version, this was a routine job, but even if it was, it gave him a very wide overview of Axis operations in the Balkans. This would have included the deportation of the Jews.

Kurt Waldheim had arrived at his new posting at Arsakli two weeks after the Jews of Salonika had begun to be sent to concentration camp. The name of the place means panorama and today it has a huge promenade terrace overlooking the whole of this major Greek port. This shows how ridiculous Waldheim's claim is that he never saw for himself the assembling of the Jews because he was in the mountains. On the eve of the war, the Jewish community of Salonika had been 65,000 strong, apart from the small groups of Jews scattered throughout the region. On January 15, 1943, Adolf Eichmann assembled officers from group E of the SD (Nazi Security Service) at Salonika, to plan the construction of a ghetto and the final deportations. Apart from Loehr, the local military commander, Max Merten, the special envoy from Bureau IX B 4 in Berlin, Dieter Wisliceny and his collaborator, Alois Brunner (Waldheim's compatriot and mastermind of the extermination of the Jews of Vienna) were in charge of implementing the plan.

A historian writing about modern Greece in an authoritative work has recorded the details. "During his trial in February-March 1959, Max Merten (who had been arrested in Greece while visiting—as a tourist!) stated that he had been "contacted" in January, 1943 not by the Obersturmbannführer SS Rolf Gunther, Eichmann's right hand man, as Wisliceny had maintained during his Nuremberg trial, but by Eichmann himself. In any case, under Order M V 1237 of 6 February 1943, the Jews of Salonika were forced to live in certain neighborhoods classified as ghettos and to wear the yellow star from the age of five. The same document, signed by Merten, delegates Wisliceny and Brunner powers of execution and indicates that the measures decided upon must be enforced by February 25 at the latest. . . .

"The deportations began on March 15, 1943. The Germans first attacked the small but very ancient Jewish communities of Florina, Verria and Langada. More than 1,000 Jews were sent in sealed boxcars to the extermination camps at Auschwitz and elsewhere. Shortly afterward, the communities of Thrace suffered the same fate. Also on March 15, the Chief Rabbi, Dr. Koretz, and the Council of the Community received the order to convert into cash all the real and movable property belonging to the Community and to put the sums thus obtained, as well as the contents of any bank accounts which they might hold , at the disposal of the German authorities. This forced sale was a unique opportunity for enrichment, not only for the Germans but also for every kind of Greek collaborator and unscrupulous speculator. According to the statements of Max Merten, the former extreme right-wing Greek Prime Minister Karamanlis and his family had a share in the spoils. Merten was tried in Salonika in 1959 but received only a token prison sentence—significantly, under Karamanlis' regime—yet after his release he did not hesitate to implicate his presumed protector.

"Of the 800,000 deportees a small number who were able to plead dual Greek and Spanish nationality, were sent to Spain. Many of them were able to stay alive until the liberation and return to their homes. The great majority of Greek Jews, however, were sent to the Auschwitz extermination camp, where they were liquidated, convoy after convoy, in the crematoria. About 5,000 Greek Jews, who were spared by Dr. Mengele, of sinister memory, were sent to Warsaw in October, 1943, where they were used to clear away the ruins of the Ghetto which had been completely destroyed by the Germans after the Jewish uprising of April 19, 1943. There they were caught up in the Polish uprising of August 1, 1944. They took part in it and were decimated in the heart of the city. The few men who survived continued to fight with the Poles by the Polski river, until the Germans were able to crush the last pockets of resistance. After the tragic end of the uprising, only a few former deportees were able to hide in a shelter they had built themselves until January 1945, at which date they were saved by the Soviet Army offensive."[30] "Even in the officers mess in Arsakli nothing was ever said about the deportation of the Jews," states Kurt Waldheim (*Der Spiegel*, April 14, 1986). This indication with its macabre (and involuntary) irony does not conform to the view of the specialists. Hagen Fleischer, a professor of German origin at the University of Crete, contends that, on the contrary, "the deportation of the 50,000 Greek Jews from Salonika which lasted until August 1943 was commented upon by ordinary German soldiers, and could not have been unknown, even to a new member of the command, especially one who enjoyed the particular esteem of his compatriot, Loehr."[31]

The tasks of locating Jews, running the ghetto and surveillance of convoys involved a lot of men, and Group Ia had its part to play. In his liaison functions with the Italian command, Waldheim dealt with the question of raids and deportations, because the German army had a great difficulty in persuading their southern allies to participate enthusiastically in *the final solution*. When they were unable to obtain a direct undertaking from the Italians to take part in operations, Wehrmacht liaison officers managed to glean information from them that was potentially useful to the German plans. Thus, on August 15, 1943 Waldheim classified and certified correct a radio message sent to him by the 1st German Alpine Division, indicating that "according to Italian reports, there are important groups of bandits in the zone southeast of the Arta.... The civilians are waiting to see what happens. Ioannina and the Jewish Committee operating in that city must be considered as the center of preparations for a resistance movement."

Elimination of Former Allies

On September 8, 1943, Italy capitulated with the Badoglio Armistice. Former colleagues had become undesirable traitors. Kurt Waldheim, who had closely followed their procrastinations, showed himself to be quite equal to his reputation as an overbearing official, his eyes fixed on duty.

On September 22, 1943 he submitted a detailed report to Oberleutant Frey (general staff of Group E) about the Italian troops still on Greek soil near Athens. He recommended that 4,600 of the 27,000 officers and men be kept in the region as a work force, and the rest sent to camps in Germany.

But there were quite a lot more Italians in the internment bases, and Waldheim's headquarters, having established a fraternal link with the Italian 11th army, simply moved in to liquidate it. *Sic transit gloria mundi.* In early October, Waldheim's superior, Major-General von Glydenfelt, announced that more than 100,000 ex-allies had been deported. And it was Waldheim who on many occasions informed headquarters how many trains would be needed for this pitiless removal![32]

According to Hagen Fleischer, "Waldheim participated in the negotiations preceding the surrender of the 11th Army. Then he personally interrogated Italian prisoners when the Germans, fearing the Italians would desert to rejoin the underground resistance movement, embarked on punitive operations to seize their former allies, as was the case in Epirus for instance, with the operation which was code-named "Operation Spaghetti."

In the rolls of Group E Command (classified secret and dated December 1, 1943) Kurt Waldheim, who had returned to Arsakli for good, appears as an O3 officer of Group Ic/AO under the direct orders of Oberleutnant Herbert Warnstorff. The military logic is very simple. There was no longer any need for an Italian interpreter. The young Austrian, who had already been entrusted with very delicate missions, was able to move on to the strategic sector of intelligence. In his self-defense in memorandum form, Kurt Waldheim emphasizes that Cell Ic had no command powers, that his days were spent in stamping "für die Richtigkeit der Ausfertigung" (certified copy) on the paperwork that passed through his office.

He certainly recalls having had one or two collaborators to help him accomplish this rather uninspiring work, but denies any constant relationship with the *Abwehr* (the German intelligence service), relying on the slant line which separates the initials "Ic" from the "AO" (*Abwehroffizier*). To put his responsibilities and his area of knowledge into context, he claims that all the important information was sent upward directly through *Abwehr* channels and not through his department. He had earlier claimed explicitly on Austrian Radio on March 25, 1986, "I was not a military intelligence officer." It thus becomes necessary to examine in detail the bureaucracy of the killing machine called the Wehrmacht.

Intelligence Officer at General Loehr's Headquarters

THE *Ic/AO* group consisted of four posts,[33] a commander, a senior officer called the O3, an "O5" officer with particular responsibility for troop morale who was assisted by a translator (who was not Waldheim) and finally the "Ic/L" officer, who was responsible for various liaison duties between the different fighting forces. Major Hammer, the official *Abwehr* representative at headquarters (according to Waldheim himself) also served as the commander, that is to say that Oberleutnant Waldheim, the O3 officer, was also directly responsible to him.

The powers of the latter, assisted by the officer Helmut Poliza, are detailed in the document entitled "Establishment of Daily Reports Morning and Evening" as being *Sonderaufgaben*, that is, *special missions*, one of those harmless-sounding Nazi names given to hide the most brutal activities, staff briefings and interrogations of prisoners. The latter task is mentioned twice, even if Kurt Waldheim subsequently denied having encountered a single·hostage or a single prisoner of war.

The Pentagon's Military Intelligence Division, having studied at length the Wehrmacht's secret reports, prepared an analysis of German military intelligence which analyzes the role of an O3 officer as follows: "He was the deputy of the chief intelligence officer. He was responsible for all operational intelligence and the control of the intelligence staff. He superintended the keeping of the situation maps and the intelligence filing system, and was responsible for informing higher and adjacent formations of all items of enemy intelligence."[34]

"I would not hesitate to state that, at least for the latter period of the Occupation, Waldheim was one of the best-informed men in the German army ... perfectly well aware of even the most insignificant aspects of the Nazi occupation of the Balkans—and it is even probable that he personally attended executions in Yugoslavia." That is the conclusion reached by Hagen Fleischer and it is hardly surprising if one considers the duties of a zealous O3—and the last thing one could reproach Kurt Waldheim with is a lack of zeal. As the man who gathered a large amount of information coming from below, the young Austrian officer was also in close contact through his work with the highest echelons of the German army in the region.

For instance, in October 1943, he posed for a photograph in the lounge of the Hotel Grande-Bretagne in Athens, in the company of Major-General Glydenfeldt, his superior, Willers, and General Felmy. He was in the center of the group but not in the foreground, just as he is in the photographic plate discovered by the Greek newspaper *To Vima*. (See photo insert.) For this reason, he was not to become one of the first to be exposed to post-war retribution. Loehr and Wisliceny were condemned to death and executed in Yugoslavia and Czechoslovakia, Eichmann was condemned to death and executed in Israel, Felmy was sentenced to 15 years imprisonment at Nuremberg, while Merten received a term of 20 years from the Greek courts, before he was claimed by the West German authorities and spent the rest of his days pleasantly in the Federal German Republic. These men were responsible for actually ordering the war crimes to be committed; Kurt Waldheim was merely responsible for having communicated all the information they needed in order to make such decisions.

The key role played by intelligence during the last phase of Hitler's war is emphasized by historians. The new regulation thought up by Colonel Liss insisted on the fact that knowledge of the enemy with his national and racial characteristics should determine all the operational choices. The Ic units were invited to transmit their information to the chief of staff directly when they thought it necessary to do so. From 1943 onward, writes David Kahn,[35] the Ic units at army corps headquarters level supplanted the intelligence units acting in the field in all the armies.

So Waldheim's unit was, like the others, granted the most extensive and effective means of action. In several zones, the historian (who, it should be noted, at the time of writing was not particularly concerned with the Waldheim affair) adds that intelligence officers "cooperated with the SS commandos, indicating to them where Jews were hidden and also sometimes themselves ordering Jews to be handed over to the SS. They received reports on the number of people killed or deported by the SS and by their own secret police operating in the sector, and filed them in their ordinary filing system along with other military documents." That was the routine. In fact, to quote the expression used by Lavroslav Kadelburg, President of the Jewish Communities of Yugoslavia, in the machinery of organizing the massacres, the O3 officer became a desk killer, a bureaucrat of terror.[36]

Before placing his signature ("W") on the documents which crossed his desk, Kurt Waldheim read them, analyzed them, filed them, compared them, and memorized them in order to ask for additional information or to pass on their contents to his chiefs. That was his job. He handled messages from operational units and from the *Abwehr*, because as David Kahn indicates, Ic at army corps level "was in charge of the men and commanders of the *Abwehr* at the front." It should be noted that German staff officers were very few, on the principle that the fewer the number of officers who were really in the know, the better.

At staff conferences, which Waldheim frequently attended, only those who had something to say were invited. "We can tell what the weather is like for ourselves," remarked an officer to explain the absence of a meteorologist at these meetings, in contrast to the practice adopted by the Allies. The members of this small team were thus not only made to work conscientiously but also with the greatest speed. One can well imagine what sort of expression would have appeared on General Loehr's face had his own O3 officer admitted to him that he had never heard of the deportation of the Jews of Salonika! Furthermore, since officers of the highest rank were constantly transferred from posting to posting, the O3 was the permanent intelligence center, the memory of the Ic/AO.

Every day, from 5:00 AM, situational reports would be sent up the hierarchical ladder of Heeresgruppe E. Three hours later, Waldheim's cell would have this important material in its possession. The process was repeated at the end of the afternoon, to establish the activity report for that day. On December 19, 1943, for instance, Kurt Waldheim knew that the Greek city of Kalavrita and the monastery of Haghia Lavra had been set on fire by German soldiers in their relentless pursuit of Communists, that on that occasion 13 monks were executed, and that in the village of Lyngiades, near Paramythia, 82 people were killed, of whom 42 were children under 15. He knew that in the town of Sparta, 128 hostages, many of whom were teachers, were shot in reprisal.

Already occupied in filing this documentation, Waldheim was also given the additional job of supervising personal matters in his unit, that is to say, spying on his colleagues and checking to see that their morale was high. On July 30, 1944 General Loehr advised his collaborators to "maintain a National-Socialist conduct," and the O3's job was to make sure this was done. The matter was all the more crucial because ten days previous, senior German officers had tried to remove Adolf Hitler. In his autobiography, Waldheim has forgotten the Balkans, but he expounds on the hopes which the attempted coup of July 20, 1944 might have aroused in him. Yet, at the time, he was actually engaged in dispelling such hopes in the consciences of his fellow workers, and denouncing them if necessary!

High Politics and Low Police

In January 1944, the Oberleutnant had thyroid problems. He obtained a 28 day sick leave on March 25, and was hospitalized in the *Heereskurlazarett* at Semmering, returning to Arsakli on about April 23. If he had merely been the easily-dispensable executive which he later described, the command could have had him replaced during his absence. Yet on May 20, Kurt Waldheim held a briefing in the presence of General Erich Schmidt-Richberg, chief of staff of Group E and second in command (after Loehr). This briefing was concerned with the situation in the Mediterranean, Italy and the Balkans, a vast survey during which the most minor details were tackled such as the use of hostages in order to ensure the protection of a train in the Peloponnese. Prisoners were to be put on board in order to deter resistance fighters from attacking it. He drew up the monthly activity report, which also covered political questions in Greece as well as an evaluation of enemy losses and an analysis of the measures taken against civilians.

To measure the scope of the subjects covered by this officer, it is sufficient to note that Waldheim countersigned a secret plan dated November 10, 1943 which aimed to oust the puppet Greek government headed by Ioannis Rallis. Installed by the Germans on April 6, 1943 to replace Logothetopoulos, whom they considered incapable of stamping out the resistance, Rallis did not, however, enjoy the complete confidence of the Nazis. The secret German report 1a Br. B 16206/43 represents him as "A former leader of the People's Party. Convinced anti-Communist. Drunkard. Appears to be Pangalos' right-hand man, Pangalos being supported by the British." His triple game (with the German occupying power, the British and the Greeks who had remained loyal to their exiled king in London) did not stop him from lending the Nazis a hand and creating the Security Battalions, a paramilitary force of native Greeks, of a type frequently established by the Nazis in the countries they occupied.

The document read by Kurt Waldheim (and only addressed to one other destination, the SS command) relates the proposal of a Greek arms dealer, Alexios Petrou, to eliminate the disgraceful Rallis government so that Nazism could triumph in Greece. Petrou, represented as an active agent of the German secret police in Salonika, had an astonishing proposal to make. If he were to become Minister of the Interior in a new government, he would do his best to exploit his close relations with the nationalist leaders to hand over the main cells of the Greek Communist Party as quickly as possible, with their heads on the block. The German police promised him that this offer would only be communicated to the competent authority, and that is what they did.

Over and above the considerations of high politics

(which, it is true, had more in common with those of a low police force), Kurt Waldheim continued to watch the deportations of the Jews. Ever since the Italian capitulation, nothing had stopped German troops from attacking the most remote communities in the Balkan Peninsula and especially in the Greek islands. Corfu, the Ionian islands, the Dodecanese, no longer benefited from the precarious protection offered them by the Italian occupation.

In July, 1944, he was informed of the deportation by ship of the Jews of Rhodes and Crete to the Auschwitz-Birkenau concentration camp. On August 11, he received a message from the Command of the Eastern Aegean about the mixed reactions of the population at the deportation of the Jews which was counterbalanced by the authorization given to take possession of Jewish goods. The Ic/AO unit, to which Kurt Waldheim belonged, not only supervised these measures, it organized them, as is witnessed in the monthly activity report of the same command, dated August 22, 1944, which stipulates, "Deportation of Jews of non-Turkish citizenship on the command's territory, according to the instructions of the High Command of Group E Ic/AO." On April 21, Ic/AO (with or without Kurt Waldheim, since there is uncertainty as to the exact date of his return to the front) sent the units concerned and the SS headquarters in Athens a detailed report on the number of Jews and foreign nationals still in Corfu.

One week later, the Korpsgruppe at Ioannina requested Waldheim's unit to discuss with the SD and the secret police the measures necessary to settle the Jewish question in the island, that is the evacuation of about 2,000 potential friends of the brave Mangeclous. On May 12, General Loehr agreed to supply additional transport for the accelerated evacuation of the Jews. On June 17, the SS estimated that 1,795 Jews from Corfu had been sent to the camps.

The "Final Solution"

In certain cases, the reports countersigned by Waldheim indicated that the Italians or Greeks who assisted in the raids considered the Germans to be savages. He himself certainly had to verify on the spot the effect of the instructions given by Eichmann or Brunner. It is impossible to confirm this with certainty, but the inspection of regional assembly centers for future deportees was quite within the scope of his responsibilities as a staff officer.

One is forced here to rely on eye-witnesses, whose evidence can only be circumstantial. Thus, on July 14 and 15, 1944, about 2,500 Jews from Rhodes were rounded up for the final solution. Three Nazi officers arrived specially to supervise operations. Maurice Soriano, who became president of the Jewish community of Rhodes, stated 40 years later that one of these men was Waldheim. The case of Ionannina is more complex. Four witnesses who survived the raid of March 25, 1944 in this northern Greek city are convinced that they recognized Kurt Waldheim as one of those present, beating hostages who did not hand over their jewels and money quickly enough. This was a young officer, tall, slim, slightly limping. It couldn't have been anyone but him, they declared, and said they were even ready to confront him. Yet if the date of the end of his hospitalization as indicated in the Semmering archives is correct, Kurt Waldheim could not have been in the town of Larissa where these deportees had been assembled.

Kurt Waldheim has not taken any notice of this evidence. He continues to maintain that he never knew anything about the deportations and in order to attenuate the flatness of his denials, he has added to his memorandum the following rider to his plea in self-defense: "I profoundly deplore the unspeakable martyrdom that was imposed on the Jewish people and I assuredly did so long before these revelations about Salonika, during my trip to Israel as well as elsewhere." Yet a man with whom he had been in close contact, Colonel Roman Loos (who was in charge of the secret police in the region) exclaimed on March 9, 1986 to a journalist from Associated Press, "What, he didn't know? But everyone knew."

In order to destroy the theories of his accusers, Kurt Waldheim has often contested the value of such eyewitnesses, whether they were Greek Jews or former Wehrmacht officers, such as those whose statements were collected by the Yugoslav War Crimes Commission. On the other hand, the candidate for the Austrian presidency considered it entirely appropriate to use the evidence of certain other eyewitnesses to justify his claim that he was not at Banja Luka during the bloody offensive in the Kozara. "The information I gathered at Arsakli was solely of a military nature," he also claims as an excuse to explain his ignorance about the fate of the Jews. Yet documents exist which prove the contrary, and particularly this completely artificial distinction between military affairs and the deportations. As far as German intelligence was concerned, they were all an integral part of the Balkan campaign.

On the subject of the "interrogation of prisoners", Kurt Waldheim chose the same attitude of systematic denial in the face of historical evidence.

Waldheim is "conciliatory". "The conciliatory man has the most difficult life imaginable. The difficulties against which he must fight can amass in such a way that while smiling he has a tragic air." Perhaps he would have preferred to tell the truth, but "at the last moment, his tongue modified the decision of his brain and instead of the truth, it emitted a nondescript phrase, rounded and polished, of an enigmatic nature, agreeable and melodious. On the Danube and on the Rhine—the two legendary rivers of Germany—such men sometimes emerged; there remained little of the Nibelungs."

Yet there are no fewer than 19 intelligence reports

signed by Kurt Waldheim himself in the U.S. National Archives which deal with details of interrogations.[37] Here again, eye witnesses exist. Ten or so former British and American POWs believe they remember Waldheim. One of them was particularly insistent. In a letter written to a British member of parliament and read out in the House of Commons on June 18, 1986, Frank Notley, a career soldier who retired in 1957 and lives in the little town of Warrington, stated, "I was taken prisoner in North Africa, and I escaped twice from internment camps in Italy and Germany. I know something about this swine Waldheim. I saw him for the first time in camp 182 in Italy. He was around when the remains of thirty or so British soldiers who had been shot were brought into camp to be buried there. The poor fellows were thrown out of the German trucks as if they were unloading sacks of manure. You can imagine for yourself the part he took in this. I saw him again in the interrogation centre where I was held."

On July 18, 1944 the Ic/AO unit indicated that on the previous day James Doughty, an American soldier, who had been captured while on a maritime reconnaissance mission had been interrogated. It should be remembered that the list of duties for Ic/AO officers states that Kurt Waldheim, the O3 officer (and his assistant) were in sole charge of interrogations. Before this, Waldheim had been engaged in dealing with various prisoners from the Anglo-American mission in Greece (according to the terms of the monthly report issued by him) and especially the seven commandos belonging to the Special Boat Squadron captured on April 7, 1944 on the little island of Alimnia, near Rhodes.

On April 27, the Ic/AO received a telegram stipulating that these men, with the exception of the British radio officer, Carpenter, and the Greek sailor, Michael Ligaris, "are to be handed over to the *Sicherheitsdienst* for a more exhaustive interrogation at the SD's convenience and afterward for special treatment in accordance with the Führer's orders." On June 5 another wire indicated that Carpenter and Ligaris "are of no more use" and that they are now to receive *Sonderbehandlung*, the notorious special treatment which simply means execution, as Hitler recommended. In fact, Hitler himself had stated in the order of the day quoted in the wire that "all the enemies captured in these so-called commando missions are to be eliminated to the last man," even if they had surrendered to the Germans.

Since he was responsible for special missions at headquarters, Waldheim must have been perfectly well aware on whom and when to inflict *Sonderbehandlung*. The only officer in the group, the British Captain Hugh Blythe, was the sole survivor who miraculously managed to live after having been sent into captivity. It should be added that one of the very few escapees, the American James Doughty, remembers having been interrogated at Arsakli, Kurt Waldheim's headquarters.

In mid-August, 1944, Kurt Waldheim received compassionate leave in order to marry Elisabeth Sissi Ritschel. About one month later, he was back at Arsakli. There were many more bitter days before the German capitulation on May 8, 1945. Right to the end, the O3 officer did his duty, having adapted since 1942 to each of the tasks to which he had been assigned.

In this regard, the future president showed such reticence in admitting the facts that one is tempted to attribute exceptionally important responsibilities to him. Certain Yugoslavs have even theorized that he participated in the negotiations between the *Abwehr* and Tito's headquarters which took place in March, 1943. On the Yugoslav side there were Milovan Djilas, Koća Popović and Vladko Velebit; on the German side, two *Abwehr* officers. General Dippold, Commander of the 717th Division, served as an intermediary and it was at his headquarters at Gornji Vakuf that the first meeting was held, the rest of the discussions taking place in Zagreb.

An exchange of prisoners was at stake, and Tito attached great sentimental importance to this fact, which explains his subsequent silence and discretion about Kurt Waldheim's past. But it is certain the head of the *Abwehr*, Admiral Canaris, had chosen trustworthy men to engage in a dialogue of which the pure and hardened Nazis officially disapproved. Milovan Djilas, whom the authors have questioned, states that he never encountered the officer Kurt Waldheim during the war.

The Yugoslav partisans, who were not, at the time, on the best of terms with either the British or the Soviets even appear to have proposed a cessation of hostilities, during these negotiations, a cessation of hostilities, on condition that they were recognized as a regular army. Ribbentrop, however, insisted that the dialogue should cease, and hostilities were resumed.

A Series of Reprisals

THEN came the fiercest obstinacy, that of the defeat. The orders communicated to Oberleutnant Kurt Waldheim do not mention any attempts at mediation or appeals for conciliation. *Total War* prevailed more than ever and if Tito, who had served in the Austrian army in 1914, had found any traces of chivalry in the behavior of the Wehrmacht, such a time was long past. The German intelligence officers became past masters in the systematic recourse to reprisals, and uncompromising terrorization of the alleged resistance fighters.

Forty years later, it is difficult in the peaceful West, used only to the exotic conflicts in the Middle East or Latin America, to imagine the huge machine that was Group E, with a strength of between 300,000–400,000 men, all bursting with the desire to manifest the greatest and most extreme cruelty.

In early October, 1944, the Headquarters of Heeres-gruppe E decided to withdraw westward; it received the order from the general command of the Balkans in Belgrade. It was there that General Wilhelm List tried right to the end to conduct a dual policy of terrorizing the local inhabitants while exploiting the internal rivalries of the resistance movements. General Loehr's team was ordered to go to Kosovska Mitrovica, where it remained until November 15, 1944. It was during this period that Kurt Waldheim became associated with the activities which led the Yugoslav War Crimes Commission to ask for his speedy extradition and trial. Kurt Waldheim became Officer O3, an expert in the art of organizing reprisals. On August 11, 1944, Kurt Waldheim indicates in his daily evening report, that the zone south of Heraklion in Crete should be considered as a sector of gang activity. Two days later, the blow was struck. In accounting to the Ic/AO for their mopping up operations, the Wehrmacht units indicated that two villages were destroyed and 20 hostages executed. At the same moment, a report countersigned by Waldheim indicates that several Communists were killed in the course of raids on Athens. On August 9, Waldheim held one of his customary briefings with General Schmidt-Richberg, during which he drew up the positive balance sheet of "Operation Viper" (*Unternehmen Kreuzotter*) which consisted of massacring whole villages to intimidate the resistors, according to the plans prepared by his own intelligence unit. On August 15, for instance, the daily report of the Ic/AO notes that the 22nd Mountain Division had "carried out exhaustive mopping up, with the destruction of all the villages, without establishing significant contact with the enemy."

The enemy, and Waldheim admitted this himself 40 years later, were the resistors. These were a very vague entity during the civil war then prevailing, as the partisans in both

Greece and Yugoslavia were riddled with internal disputes which the Germans tried to exploit to the maximum. Twelve Nazi officers, including General List, were convicted at the Nuremberg Trials (August 18, 1947) for the crimes they had committed during Operation Viper.

For months the Germans had danced to the tune of total vengeance, using an iron hand; the senior officers of the Wehrmacht had no choice. They had to advance, even in retreat, and prepare the ground for saving their own skins by eliminating an enemy which, despite its incoherences and its schisms, would not let itself be beaten. It was here, in Kurt Waldheim's zone of operations, that Curzio Malaparte discovered the Nazi attitude to war: "I found myself outside the village of Rita, near Panchevo outside Belgrade, and was waiting to cross the Danube.... An SS detachment was awaiting the order to force their way across the river. One of them was sitting near the place where I sat myself.... He told me that the recruits of the SS Leibstandart were trained to bear the pain of others without flinching. I repeat that those blue eyes were extraordinarily pure. The recruits had to hold a cat in the left hand and by the skin of the neck so that its paws were free to defend itself, while using their right hands to cut out its eyes with a small knife. That is how one learns to kill the Jews."[38]

Crime at the End of the Road

REPRISALS became the watchword of German military strategy when the headquarters to which Kurt Waldheim belonged withdrew to Kosovska Mitrovica, south of Belgrade. It was then that the events took place which in 1947 would justify the verdict of the Yugoslav War Crimes Commission, directed by Professor Dusan Nedljković (who died before the

Waldheim affair broke, but whose integrity is recognized in contemporary Yugoslavia). The verdict was murder.

The rather disorganized nature of the revelations made in 1986 about Kurt Waldheim's past, even the complexity of the case, might have caused this important point to be neglected. The post- war Yugoslav indictment deals solely with events which occurred between October 1944 and May 1945. Not that the actions of the Wehrmacht lieutenant, who later became an O3 officer, were harmless; they were sufficiently serious for the perpetrator to want to conceal them for 40 years. They explain the part he admits to having played in the Nazi enterprise. Yet the official inquiry, led by an independent commission whose credibility has never been in doubt, concentrated on only a very short period in Waldheim's hidden years.

It all began on October 12, 1944, when Kurt Waldheim's daily reports make two mentions of the worrying presence of partisans in the stretch of road between Stip and Kočane. This did not cease to alarm him, because this was the withdrawal route westward from Arsakli. Kurt Waldheim confirmed that he had reached Kosovka Mitrovica by air on October 13, and cites as confirmation for this Captain Prem, the pilot's, log and witnesses. These proofs have not been established and it is known that some of the command traveled by road. On October 14 (not October 20, as Waldheim claims today), German soldiers burned three villages in the zone which O3 pinpointed for them, Krupiste, Gorni Balvan and Dolnyi Balvan. This was no act of desperate rage, but a carefully-planned reprisal. One hundred fourteen people were executed, swelling the balance sheet of enemy losses which Kurt Waldheim drew up at the end of October. It read, 739 killed, 94 taken prisoner. Were all of them "bandits"? The balance sheet only lists 63 weapons (13 of them machine guns) as having been seized.

Captain Karl Heinz Egberts-Hilker, head of the

reconnaissance patrol of the 22nd Infantry Division, admitted to the Yugoslav judges his responsibility for the massacres of October 14, and he was condemned to death in 1948. His evidence appears in the Yugoslav War Crimes Commission file concerning Kurt Waldheim. In his memorandum, the latter pretends not to know the identity of this officer, on the pretext that his name is sometimes incorrectly reproduced as Egberts or Eckbert-Hilker. Yet the captain clearly stated that he had acted according to the reprisals principles laid down by Hitler (the order previously recalled in this chapter) and on the recommendations as elaborated by Waldheim's Ic/AO section. Curiously, Egberts-Hilker's evidence has disappeared from the International War Crimes Commission files preserved in the U.N. Archives and unearthed in 1986.

Yet the three martyred villages are not the only basis for the Yugoslav complaints. When in 1948, the Allies accepted the Yugoslav request, they indicated on the file that the acts of which Waldheim was accused took place in all parts of Yugoslavia.

The original version of the Yugoslav dossier, as it was communicated to the journalists of *Vecernje Novosti* in Belgrade, states as follows: "The crimes cited here involve the 297th Division in Macedonia, which in November 1944 set fire to the villages of Svinista and Openića, killing several people. In May, 1944, the troops burned down the village of Popoveć. The 41st Division, also in Macedonia, executed many peasants in September nd October, and burned the villages of Smoljare (4 people executed), Gabrovo (2), Petrovo (2), Rusinovo, Radoviste, Zlesevo, Zubovo (9 people shot). And the crimes committed by the troops of the 22nd Infantry Division in western Bosnia in early 1945 were in the village of Glumin where 11 people were executed, Kozluk and Tbanovice (6), Snagovo (8), Colopak (12), Divic (7) and Kostirjevo (6)." As many crimes as this were listed, in addition to the incidents on the road between Stip and Kočane.

The Yugoslav investigators add: "The evidence presented above establishes that these orders were planned in detail with the cooperation of the Ic unit at the army corps headquarters, and in particular with the collaboration of Lieutenant Waldheim. The execution of these orders devolves an even greater responsibility on those who ordered them and transmitted them to the lower ranks [of the army]".

Here is the crux of the matter. There are five witnesses to reinforce the indictments of the Yugoslav commission. They are Klaus Melinschoff, who belonged to General Loehr's command, and who confirmed that Waldheim was assistant to the head of intelligence services; Johann Mayer, who was responsible for manpower at the same headquarters, who emphasized that Waldheim's task was "to offer suggestions for reprisals, the fate of prisoners of war and imprisoned civilians"; and he recalls that "some of the people executed at Sarajevo in November 1944 received this treated as the result of an order given by Waldheim in reprisal for the desertion from the German army of several other men." (Would these have been anti-Communist nationalists, Albanians from Kosovo enrolled in the heyday of the occupation?) In addition to Captain Egberts-Hilker's evidence, there is the evidence of Robert Voight, a young officer in Waldheim's division, and of Marcus Hartner, a cartographer. The latter drew up a detailed and precise flow-chart for the Yugoslav investigators which indicated the tasks of each officer in the headquarters. "In view of the evidence given, the Official War Crimes Commission rules that Lieutenant Waldheim is a war criminal, whose extradition to Yugoslavia is requested." On December 12, 1947, the Waldheim file was completed by the commission and numbered F-25 572. The cover is inscribed "Murders and massacres, executions of hostages, destruction of goods by fire." The Allied Commission for its part, retained the following indictments on February 19, 1948: "Putting hostages to death, murder". For the direct witnesses of history, Yugoslav or other, the mere scope of Kurt Waldheim's job at headquarters was sufficient to prove that the reprisals were conducted on his recommendation. Other documents which support this contention exist in Yugoslavia, in private archives. The Belgrade magazine *Intervju* could thus state in June, 1986 that "Kurt Waldheim coordinated Nazi reprisals operations in Yugoslavia between mid-October, 1944 and May, 1945." According to this bi-monthly publication, Waldheim stayed long enough at Kosovska Mitrovica to supervise all the reprisals actions taken in the province of Kosovo, and he continued to do so as Heeresgruppe E moved westward.

The Riddle of the Surrender

Until April, 1944 there are still traces of written evidence to show that Oberleutnant Kurt Waldheim pursued his normal activities. But the crisis was approaching, confusion increased in the field and it is difficult to follow his tracks. Yet were it known what route he took during the last days of the war, it would clear up a lot of later mysteries. According to him (still in the self-defense he published on April 12, 1986, but also in a number of his statements to the press) he remained with General Loehr's command at least until April 20, 1944, in the city of Agram. He then received the order to rejoin an infantry division based not far from Trieste.

"At that moment," he writes, "a number of officers and soldiers posted to the command were transferred to the operational units, even if, as in my case, they had been declared unfit for service in combat units." To reach Trieste, Waldheim would have had to pass north of Klagenfurt (in Austrian Carinthia), and would have stumbled into the enemy lines while trying to turn southward again. He would then have had to turn northward toward the German positions "to inform them that he [was unable to] reach [his] posting". It was then that he learned of the surrender and hastened to join his family by crossing the Styrian Alps to the north.

As usual, Kurt Waldheim presents his version of events with the greatest candor, as if this tale of his flight from the Balkans was not provided 40 years later, during which time he had concealed his very presence in Yugoslavia and Greece. Since the order transferring him to Trieste has never been found, it is impossible to accept without question a story which seems strange on at least one point. It is hard to see why General Loehr would have separated himself from his intelligence cell at the very time when superior knowledge of the field was most required in order to make a successful getaway, and where the disputes among the Yugoslav resistance needed to be exploited to the full in order to try and save his own skin.

From November 15, 1944 through February, 1945, Loehr's headquarters remained in Sarajevo, and then withdrew to Zagreb. His staff remained on Yugoslav soil until the last moment, because the partisans were able to arrest some of them. On May 7, 1945 a delegation of Yugoslav partisans presented themselves at Loehr's headquarters near Zagreb, at Sevnica, in order to begin negotiations for the surrender of the German forces. One of those who attended these meetings, Reserve Captain Milan Skero, is adamant: Oberleutnant Waldheim was still with General Loehr at that date.

Vladimir Dedijer, Tito's biographer, and a former colonel in the partisans, Director of the Yugoslav Information Service at the Liberation, member of the Russell Tribunal since 1966, holds no fewer than 244 military documents which directly or indirectly implicate Oberleutnant Waldheim. As far as he is concerned, as well—he told us as much in June,

1986—it is certain that the young Austrian officer was still with Loehr on the eve of the German surrender. This is also believed by Bogdan Kryzsman, a specialist in the history of Croatia, who told us of his theory that Kurt Waldheim was briefly taken prisoner by the Yugoslav partisans before being able to escape.

In fact, the circumstances of the surrender of Loehr and his staff remain confused. The Austrian general certainly signed the capitulation document in the presence of the Yugoslav emissaries, but he immediately broke his promise and forced his way toward southern Austria, which was under Anglo-American control. When he and his men reached Plinberg, he surrendered to the British, who did not seem too eager to hand him back to the Yugoslavs. It was two years before he was to be handed over to a Yugoslav court which ordered him to be hanged.

Witnesses have confirmed that on or about May 15, 1945, Kurt Waldheim was in the Austrian village of Stervja, in the Ramsau district, where his wife had just given birth to their daughter. In any case, it is certain that the Allies, even if they allowed him this freedom, were keeping an eye on him. From the end of May to the beginning of August, 1945, he was interned in the American camp at Bad Toelz, in upper Bavaria. It was then that the deal was struck which allowed the young Oberleutnant to begin a new life. In exchange for information (and he had plenty to offer!), he was authorized to return to Vienna and act as though nothing had happened since 1942.

On August 30, he appeared at the Vienna Superior Court to receive his post as lawyer trainee. On November 26, having practiced at the Court in the Baden district, he entered the Department of Foreign Affairs in the Austrian Federal Chancellory. His brief posting to Baden (near Vienna) where his father was living shows how much he had already been exonerated, since that city is in the zone which was under Soviet control and he was quite unafraid of going there.

The hidden years were forgotten, only five months after the German defeat. This sudden amnesia of hundreds of Austrians compromised by the war has escaped historic investigation until now. The question is actually taboo in a country whose redemption in the eyes of the world is based on a lie. In the words of Ecclesiasticus, "it is better to be a thief than a persistent liar," though he also says, "The heart of man is more wary than seven watchmen on the watchtower."

3

The lie, a way of life

You did this, my memory tells me.
You didn't do it, says my pride.
In the end, my pride wins.
Nietsche

In December, 1947, the Yugoslav War Crimes Commission reached its conclusions, which were damning for Kurt Waldheim. It now had to obtain a guarantee from the Allied Commission, because the man they sought was in another country, under the joint protection of Great Britain, the United States, France, and the Soviet Union, the guardian powers of the Second Austrian Republic.

On December 25, the Chairman of the Yugoslav Commission, Professor Dusan Nedljković, transmitted the file to the Yugoslav legation in London where the Allied investigators were based. It was accompanied by a detailed letter. Waldheim's case would be dealt with particularly quickly because the reports about it were complete and sufficient. He knew that Kurt Waldheim "is today in Austria, and is not only a free man but even occupies the post of Secretary at the Ministry of Foreign Affairs."

Then came the first link in a staggering chain of bureaucratic blunders and official negligence. The Yugoslav representative in Vienna was never informed of this development. Bogdan Kryzsman, who was Secretary at the Yugoslav legation in the Austrian capital until 1948 has told us that his attention was never drawn to the Waldheim case. Waldheim himself, whom he worked with almost daily, displayed the greatest courtesy toward Kryzsman; he was careful never to mention to the emissary of the hated partisans those three years he had just spent in the Balkans. He never made the slightest allusion to it.

The United Nations War Crimes Commission, then based in London, which brought together the representatives of 17 countries under British chairmanship,[39] analyzed the Yugoslav application quite quickly. It was not rejected. According to Yugoslav historian Vladimir Dedijer, 75% of the several hundreds of requests for prosecution submitted by Yugoslavia were considered unjustified in London.

On February 19, 1948 the Waldheim case (R/N/684) was classified "A", i.e. having priority. The first page of the file which bears the heading "United Nations War Crimes Commission" and the registration number 7744/4/G/557, states that the man is to be prosecuted for "putting hostages to death and murder," for "Violation of Articles 23 b & c, 46 and 50 of the Hague Regulations, 1907, and Article 3, para. 3 of the Law concerning Crimes against the People and the State, 1945."

The summary of incriminating facts reads as follows: "Oberleutnant WALDHEIM, the German Abwehrofficier with the Ic staff of the 'Heeresgruppe E', headed by General LOEHR, is responsible for the retaliation actions carried out by the Wehrmacht units in Yugoslavia, inasmuch as the 'Heeresgruppe E' was involved in directing the retaliation orders issued by the OKW (Wehrmacht General Command). Thus the Ic. staff of the 'Heeresgruppe E' were the means for the massacre of numerous sections of the Serb population." Curiously, the Allied services considered that Kurt Waldheim's address at the time was unknown, although he was certainly not difficult to find.

While his name was recalled in high places, the young demobilized officer worked very hard to obtain his certificate of political virginity, at a time when de-Nazification was fashionable. In August, 1945 he was able to obtain a certificate stating that he had always behaved as an anti-Nazi. He got this from the branches of the two main Austrian political parties, the Socialist Party and the Austrian People's Party.

On November 3, he admitted on an official form that he had been a member of the SA cavalry corps. Three weeks later, he entered the Austrian Ministry of Foreign Affairs as a trainee. The regular de-Nazification procedures used in Austria were applied to him—or rather, began to be applied. File Sk 235 was opened on him at the provincial Superior

Court, but the inquiry initiated on the subject of his activities from 1938 onward stopped on June 29 when Kurt Waldheim officially joined the staff of the Ministry of Foreign Affairs.

Kurt Waldheim cannot claim, as he has done 40 years later, that the administrative inquiry absolved him of any blame. It was the officials of the Austrian ministry who cut short this inquiry when they decided to employ him and thus make official his full reinstatement into normal life.

The Pardon: An Administrative Formality

At the time, Austria was not a member of the United Nations Organization. They joined in 1955 after the inception of the State Treaty. Contact between Austrian officials and the allied powers was made far more often through the relations established between the Resistance and the Allies than through normal diplomatic channels. Personal contacts and ties between the secret services were used to establish the new Austrian apparatus of state. (The uneasy and tense atmosphere that then prevailed in Vienna is brilliantly re-created by Graham Greene in *The Third Man*.)

Kurt Waldheim sought a job which would measure up to his ambitions. He presented himself at the office of the Minister of Foreign Affairs, Karl Gruber. He was received by the Minister's secretary, Fritz Molden, who had served as a liaison between the Austrian resistance and the Allies during the war. He was married to the daughter of Allen Dulles, head of the American secret service in Europe, the OSS, predecessor of the CIA. Molden, 27, was the same age as Waldheim. He knew that rumors were circulating in Vienna about this young man, but he did not attach much importance to them. "He was no hero," he said of Kurt Waldheim, defending him when the question arose again in 1986. But the "grand coalition" then in power (Socialists, Communists and Catholics of the People's Party) were looking for competent and dedicated men rather than heros.[40] Like Gruber, like most senior Austrian civil servants, Molden knew that most of the electorate had once accepted the Anschluss, that more than 500,000 of them had belonged to Nazi organizations, and that it was dangerous to deepen the rift between the various political factions which emerged from the resistance and this deep country. This situation was described by Karl Gruber in his memoirs in 1963.[41]

"The political ups and downs since 1918," wrote Gruber, "had caused irreparable damage to the Austrian diplomatic corps. In 1918, many Monarchists were forced to resign. In 1934, the Socialists were removed from responsible positions. In 1938, it was the turn of he Christians and any Austrian patriots who had no political affiliations. Finally, in 1945, the National Socialists disappeared. The result was that only an infinitesimal number of officials were still employed who had worked right from 1918 to 1945.... Most of the staff of the Ministry of Foreign Affairs were untrained and inexperienced. They almost had to be picked up off the streets. The younger generation had a very poor knowledge of languages, as a consequence of being cut off from the outside world by the war and the occupation."

Yet what this diplomat refrains from saying in this depressing picture of the *Ballhausplatz*, the Austrian equivalent of the State Department building, is that just after the war there were plenty of competent, bilingual men who had returned to Vienna. These were the emigrants who had been forced to leave by the Nazi regime. However, for political reasons, he made sure they were barred from entry into the diplomatic corps. It was better to recruit a Kurt Waldheim with his doubtful past than an emigrant whose past was irreproachable but who would be difficult to control politically.

In making this choice, he received the tacit approval of the Allies. At Gruber's request, Molden in fact officially questioned the political police, the Minister of the Interior—a Socialist, Oskar Helmer, and especially those responsible for Allied counter-espionage. The latter, in particular, considered the moral considerations of the Commission in London to be useless luxuries. It was all right for the biggest fish to be caught in the net of the Nuremberg Trials, but in the field, one had to use men whose past was more or less troubled. The gap widened between those who wanted to apply just desserts to the crimes committed and those who wanted to restore the institutions swept away by the Nazi hurricane in Europe as quickly as possible. The two paths of logic, two moral codes, confronted each other. "Realism" won the day. In that sense, the Waldheim case is a classic example of the history of this century.

Unsuccessful De-Nazification

THE Waldheim affair provoked a considerable misunderstanding between the majority of Austrian public opinion and the rest of the world. A people suddenly felt themselves to be under brutal attack, singled out, collectively returned to their darkest hour, to a past which they are determined to forget. In fact, only the closest observers of political life and the intellectual scene in Austria had studied this extraordinary collective amnesia, the large-scale repression which has taken place in Vienna, of the *Vergangenheitsbewaltigung* (overcoming the past) which the German Federal Republic made the major theme of public debate after 1945.

The calm certainty of collective innocence which prevailed among most Austrians was hardly affected by the various incidents which preceded the polemics about Kurt

Waldheim. The country overcame the Peter scandal in 1971 without a major crisis. Peter was the former chairman of the Freedom Party (FPÖ), an ex-colonel in the SS suspected of having participated in the mass executions of partisans and Jews on the eastern front. He was to become Speaker of the Austrian parliament with the support of Chancellor Kreisky and had to stop campaigning for the post after a campaign against him conducted by the Nazi-hunter Simon Wiesenthal.

Animosity between Bruno Kreisky and Simon Wiesenthal dates from this period. Now there's a new disagreement between the two men over Kurt Waldheim. While the former chancellor spectacularly declared in April, 1986 that "he was breaking his long friendship" with the former UN Secretary-General, Wiesenthal actually supported Kurt Waldheim, at least in the beginning, essentially because of his own hostility to the Socialist Party.

More recently, in 1985, the welcome which Minister of Defense Friedhelm Frischenschlager, gave to the Nazi war criminal Walter Reder, who was released from Italian prisons after many decades of incarceration, at the very moment when the World Jewish Congress was holding its general meeting in Vienna, did not cause a government crisis between the Socialist Party and the Freedom Party, of which the Minister of Defense was a member.

Since 1945, Austria has become accustomed to seeing former Nazi leaders come back into prominence, trusted by all the political parties. Of course, most were members of the Freedom Party, whose avowed objective was to win over former Nazi party members. One of the founders, Anton Reinthaler, had been Secretary of State in the ephemeral Austrian government led by the Nazi Arthur Seiss-Inquart just after the Anschluss, but there were even members of the People's Party and the Socialist Party (SPÖ). For instance, Leopold Wagner, one of the leading lights in the SPÖ and

Chairman of the Carinthian Regional Council, has never concealed the fact that the he was a national leader of the Hitler Youth.

In the eyes of the majority of Austrians, therefore, Kurt Waldheim's past in no way constitutes an obstacle to his rise to power. He is rather less marked than some other political and economic leaders in Austria, and at first appeared as someone who merely did his duty, just like millions of his compatriots. If he is declared guilty in the eyes of universal morals, a whole nation stands condemned at the bar of history.

The prevailing attitude in Austria a few months after the Presidential election was that Kurt Waldheim's only mistake consisted in not having gallantly owned up to his past. He sought to distort the truth to extract himself from the situation in which so many found themselves, and he established his career on the image of the anti-Nazi that he never was. The perception of Nazism in the Austrian collective conscience has nothing to do with the way it is perceived in other countries, including the German Federal Republic. There is far greater emphasis on the misfortunes which Austria suffered after its defeat, and little attempt to analyze the monstrous nature of the totalitarian system for which a large part of the population acted as agents, either through the herd instinct or by conscious and enthusiastic choice.

"We were the first victims of Nazism." This refrain which has become the historical creed of contemporary Austria is based upon the famous Moscow declaration made on November 1, 1943, and signed by the US Secretary of State and the Ministers of Foreign Affairs of the USSR and Great Britain. The text of this declaration has played a major part in the subsequent misinterpretation of Austria's role in World War II and its attendant atrocities.

The declaration states: "The Governments of the United Kingdom, the Soviet Union and the United States of America agree to consider that Austria, the first free country to fall victim to Hitlerite aggression, must be freed from German domination. They consider the annexation of Austria by Germany, proclaimed on March 15, 1938 as null and void. They do not consider themselves bound in any way by the changes made in Austria since that date. They declare that they would like to see the establishment of a free and independent Austria, and to this end they would like to smooth the path leading the Austrians, like their neighbors confronted with the same problems, toward political and economic security which is the only foundation for a lasting peace. Austria must, however, be reminded that it bears a responsibility from which it cannot escape for its participation in the war on the side of Hitlerite Germany, and that it is indispensable to take into account, in the final reckoning, its own efforts to liberate itself."

This declaration was written at a time when nothing seemed less certain than the rapid victory of the Allies over Hitler; today, Austria only wants to remember the first part of the declaration. When one reads the entire document, and especially when it is placed in the context of the political and military situation of late 1943, it acquires a completely different meaning.

This declaration is, above all, an invitation to the Austrians to revolt against Nazi domination, and was designed to weaken the hinterland of the Reich, whose troops were still advancing deep into the East and were in control of the West, eight months before the Normandy landings. It was part of the psychological warfare and was designed to show the Austrians that they had extenuating circumstances should they decide to become turncoats to any significant extent.

The Austrian Sense of Duty

THE declaration certainly did not produce any spectacular results. Unlike the neighboring countries referred to in the text, especially Yugoslavia, Czechoslovakia and Hungary, there was little significant Austrian armed resistance to Nazism until the very last days, when defeat seemed inevitable. Then groups of resistance fighters emerged, principally in the Tyrol, where the arrival of the Allies was welcomed by covering towns and villages with the red and white flag of their refound independence.

Even these were only isolated incidents. Most Austrians, did their duty right up to the last moment, as did Kurt Waldheim's predecessor, President Rudolf Kirschläger, a captain in the Wehrmacht, who did not hesitate to send young adolescents, the last reserves of the Reich's army, to be massacred by the Soviet tanks at the gates of Vienna on the eve of the surrender.

Once the defeat was accomplished, the occupying powers found themselves faced with an impossible problem. They had to simultaneously rid the country of all the elements which had been most compromised by Nazism while maintaining the fiction of an Austria that had been a victim of Hitler's annexation. Each of the Allied powers arrived with their own ideas of how de-Nazification should be carried out. The Soviets were first and foremost anxious to flush out the criminals who had operated on their territory during the black days of the German advance; the Americans and British arrived armed with theories conceived in exile by German and Austrian emigrants, most of them Marxist-inspired, who viewed in Nazism the alliance of capital with the forces of nationalism and reaction.

Austria, unlike Germany, was submitted to a special de-Nazification procedure. The *ad hoc* committees did not

consist solely of members of the occupation forces. Through
the intermediary of the three permitted political parties in
1945—the People's Party, the Socialists and the Communists—
the Austrians were also in charge of the purification, and
negotiated on a case-by-case basis the fate which awaited
those who were compromised by Nazi rule.

The occupation authorities were merely there to supervise the smooth running of the process. Yet due to their poor
knowledge of the terrain, they were generally hoodwinked by
the Austrian committees, whose members, whatever their
political persuasions, knew very well that they would have to
live in future alongside the very people whom they had to
judge. If, during the first phase of the de-Nazification which
lasted for barely a year (from April, 1945 to January, 1946),
there were internments, removals from office, even trials and
death sentences of the most severely compromised elements,
the main work of these de-Nazification committees soon began
to consist essentially of finding the best ways in which to whitewash the individuals under their jurisdiction. Implicit bargaining was taking place under the noses of the occupying powers.
"Give me a certificate for such-and-such a member of my
party and I'll whitewash such-and-such a member of yours...."

It isn't surprising then that Kurt Waldheim never had
any difficulty in obtaining a certificate classifying him as one
of the uncompromised from the provisional authorities in
Lower Austria. The whole art of the Austrian representatives
on these commissions consisted in allowing the maximum
number of individuals to escape punishment, in the hope that
the electorate would be grateful to them for it. Naturally, this
does not mean that no one at all was held to account. About
40 people were sentenced to death and thousands of others
were imprisoned; many were barred from holding public
office, and students who had become too involved in Nazism
were banned from continuing their studies. All this marked

This photo shows a group of German army officers on leave in 1943 at the Hotel Grande-Bretagne in Athens. Kurt Waldheim is (1), at the back. He was an associate of General Glydenfelt (2), Lieutenant-Colonel Willers (3) and General Helmut Felmy (4). Felmy, who had been commander-in-chief of southern Greece (from June, 1941 to August, 1942) then commander of the 68th army corps (from June, 1943 to October, 1944) was sentenced at the Nuremburg Trials in 1948 to fifteen years imprisonment for war crimes.

This photo was taken on May 22, 1943 at Podgorica (now Titograd) airport in the province of Montenegro, Yugoslavia. Of the four men, Kurt Waldheim is second from the left, and the Italian general Escola Roncaglia is fourth from the left (Photo WJC)

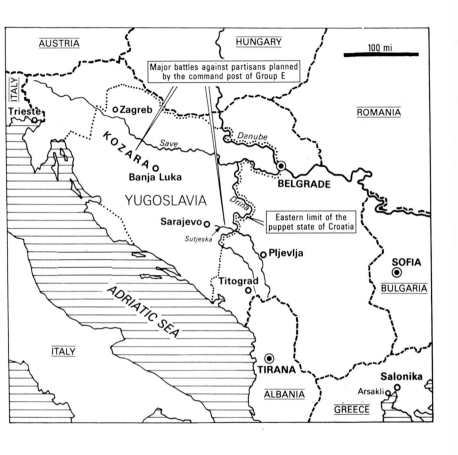

Yugoslavia during the Balkan Wars of the "interpreter" Kurt Waldheim.

UNITED NATIONS WAR CRIMES COMMISSION

YUGOSLAV CHARGES AGAINST GERMAN WAR CRIMINALS

0240 4/14   CASE No. R/N/684.

Name of accused, his rank and unit, or official position. (Not to be translated.)	Kurt(?) WALDHEIM, Oberleutnant. Abwehrofficier with the Ic - Abteilung des Generalstabes der Heeresgruppe E from April 1944 until the capitulation of Germany. (F.25572)
Date and place of commission of alleged crime.	From April 1944 - May 1945. All parts of Yugoslavia.
Number and description of crime in war crimes list.	II. Putting Hostages to Death. I. Murder.
References to relevant provisons of national law.	Violation of Articles 23 b & c, 46 and 50, of the Hague Regulations, 1907, and Article 3, para. 3 of the Law concerning Crimes against the People and the State, 1945.

SHORT STATEMENT OF FACTS.

Oberleutnant WALDHEIM, the German Abwehrofficier with the Ic. staff of the "Heeresgruppe E", headed by General LOEHR, is responsible for the retaliation actions carried out by the Wehrmacht units in Yugoslavia, inasmuch as the "Heeresgruppe E" was involved in directing the retaliation orders issued by the OKW. Thus the Ic. staff of the "Heeresgruppe E" were the means for the massacre of numerous sections of the Serb population.

In 1948, the United Nations War Crimes Commission was informed by Yugoslavia of the case of Kurt Waldheim. He was accused of having committed two war crimes between April, 1944 and May, 1945 on Yugoslav soil. The two indictments retained, in the order in which they appear on the document, are: "II. Putting Hostages to Death" and "I. Murder" (Photo WJC)

This photo was taken on May 1, 1938 during a meeting organized by Gauleiter Bürckel, shortly after the Anschluss, on the Heldenplatz in Vienna. It shows a group of National Socialist students on parade wearing the uniform of their organization. Kurt Waldheim is one of them (marked with a cross). When shown this photo, he claimed that it must have been his double. (Photo: WJC)

▲
This is the individual file card of the Reich's Ministry of Justice completed by Kurt Waldheim in 1940. Section 8 deals with "political memberships" and section 8-b concerns "mass movements." Kurt Waldheim replies with three claims, "SA Cavalry Group 5/90, SA ("Brownshirt") member since November 18, 1938, NS (Nazi) Student Organization since April 1, 1938" (Private collection.)

On November 3, 1945, Kurt Waldheim completed a "Personal Registration Form". Under "membership of NSDAP [Nazi] organizations", he merely replies, in contrast to his reply in 1940: "NS Reiterkops" [National Socialist Cavalry Corps]. He does not indicate, as requested in the questionnaire, his date of entry nor the length of time he was a member. Under the heading "Funktionen" (responsibilities), he replies "none." Above the signature, the form indicates that these replies are sworn. (Private collection) ▶

Personenstandesblatt

für die Meldung von Beamten und Angestellten beim m

Bezirksgericht Baden bei Wien

Raum für Lichtbild

Zuname:	Dr. WALDHEIM
Vorname:	Kurt
Titel:	Assessor (K)
Geboren am:	21.12.1918
Geburtsort (Land):	St.Andrä-Wördern , N.Oesterr.

Wehrverbände der NSDAP (SS, SA, NSKK, NSFK), Eintrittstag, Zeitraum der Dauer:	NS-Reiterkorps.
Letzte Dienststelle:	
Funktionen:	keine.
Anmerkung:	

Wien, am 3.11. 1945.

Die wahrheitsgetreue Beantwortung obiger Fragen bestätige ich an Eldes Statt mit meiner eigenhänc Unterschrift:

Dr. Waldheim

This photo, published on the front page of the Wehrmacht newspaper for the Balkan front, shows General Alexander Loehr (condemned to death and hanged in Yugoslavia after the war) surrounded by his closest collaborators at Arsakli, in Greece, in 1943. General Loehr (wearing glasses) is leaning over the map. Kurt Waldheim, his "O3" intelligence officer, is the fourth man at the back. (Photo WJC)

the initial phase of de-Nazification in Austria. The Austrian Ambassador in Paris, in a letter to the newspaper *Le Monde* on the day after Kurt Waldheim's election, was able to quote statistics which showed that de-Nazification in his country had produced a certain amount of results. Yet when the figures are examined more closely, as they were by the committee of historians who met in Vienna in March, 1985 on the initiative of the Viennese Institute for Science and Art, they provide a different view of Austria's relationship to its Nazi past.

Once the storm had passed, the whole country's energy was devoted to implementing the amnesties which, beginning in 1948, completely nullified the effects of the de-Nazification of the early days. The Catholic church, and especially the Archbishop of Salzburg, Monsignor Rohrbacher, was busy protecting former Nazis, to the extent where a joke began to circulate in that city where Mozart was born, "Do you need proof that Hitler is really dead? Well here it is. If he were still alive, Cardinal Rohrbacher would have taken him under his wing."

At a deeper level, the influence of National Socialist ideology remained amazingly strong among the population, as witnessed in 1948 by a public opinion survey, one of the first of the type, carried out by the American occupation troops. Three years after the Third Reich had disintegrated, more than 40% of the population believed that National Socialism had been a good idea that had been badly put into practice, as against 41% who thought it had been a bad idea.

The Normalization of Nazism

A DASH to the polls by former Nazi Party members who were allowed to take part in the 1949 elections put a definitive end to any attempt to root out the stigmata of Nazism in a country which aspired above all to retain its newly-gained normality.

The characteristically provincial pettiness of the new rulers of the country came to the fore when the question of compensation for the Austrian victims of Nazis was raised. West German Chancellor Konrad Adenauer made it a point of honor to grant substantial reparations to the victims and to the State of Israel, seeing this gesture as the condition for his country's reinstatement among the civilized nations of the world. Yet when his Austrian counterpart, Chancellor Julius Raab, received Nahum Goldmann, founder of the World Jewish Congress and Chairman of the Claims Conference, the body empowered to negotiate with the countries concerning the reparations due to the persecuted Jews, he greeted him with the words, "Jews and Austrians are both the victims of Nazism!" Nahum Goldmann replied, "Yes, Herr Chancellor, that is why I have come to ask you how much money the Jews owe the Austrians." Nahum Goldmann had the greatest possible difficulty in persuading the Austrians to admit that the Second Republic ought to be responsible for the liabilities for the Hitler period. The reparations paid by Austria to survivors of the Holocaust were far smaller than those awarded to German Jews and only began to be paid in the early 1960s.

For the Austrians, there was no break between the past and the present. Many consider that having been a Nazi means to many that one held an opinion that was no less respectable than any other, and that the Nazi party is only one of the elements responsible for Austria's misfortunes between 1938 and 1945.

At the very height of the Waldheim affair, one of the most influential editorial writers in the Austrian press did not hesitate to write in the *Kronenzeitung* dated May 4, 1986, under the headline "Anachronism", "We have reached the stage where the former National Socialists, who were so heavily condemned on the basis of laws of doubtful legality, have begun to realize that the acts committed by the other parties responsible for the downfall of Austrian democracy have remained unpunished. That is why they consider themselves to be have been sufficiently punished and no longer see any reason why they should cover themselves in sackcloth and ashes. Even less so, when yesterday's victors have broken their promises and have themselves committed the same crimes of which the Germans were convicted...." This passage is not extracted from some private neo-Nazi publication, but was published in the form of an editorial by the Austrian daily with the biggest circulation—900,000 copies in a country of 8 million inhabitants.

It is by no means the least significant of the consequences of the Waldheim affair to have exposed the mentality of the Austrian public, a mentality which encourages the efforts of the revisionist historians in the Western world, a mentality which excuses Nazism on the grounds that it was basically run-of-the-mill totalitarianism, and that the atrocities committed in its name were comparable with those committed by other types of regime.

The responsibility for the failure to de-Nazify Austria certainly does not rest solely with the Austrians. Shortly after they arrived in the country, the Allies proved themselves to be far more concerned with scoring points off each other in the Cold War which was then in its early stages, than in supervising the regeneration of an Austria infected with the poison of Nazism. The French bear a particularly heavy responsibility in this respect. Their occupation zone in the Tyrol and Vorarlberg was the one in which de-Nazification was at its mildest, The commander-in-chief of the French occupation forces in Austria, General Béthouart, owed a large measure of his popularity which still survives in Austria to this day to his efforts to defend the amnesty proposals against those Allies who were a little more cautious ... The occupying powers, all of whom belong to the UN Security Council, were thus directly responsible from the beginning for Kurt Waldheim having been able to "sail through" de-Nazification.

The Yugoslav Double Game

K<small>URT</small> Waldheim was even able to dodge the Yugoslav aspect of his case. World War II brought out the worst fratricidal conflicts and the bitterest national quarrels in that country. The Croats were pitted against the Serbs, the Albanians of Kosovo chose the Nazi camp in defiance of the central Yugoslav authority, the Titoist Communists fought against the Cetnik nationalists led by Draza Mihailović, the so-called "King of the Mountains". Tramcars ran in Zagreb on which Serbs, Jews, Gypsies and dogs were forbidden to ride. Ante Pavelić, the Croatian henchman of the Nazis, told Hitler on June 7, 1941, "We are not Slavs, we are of Gothic origin."

Tito was well aware that in order to firmly establish his federal power he could not reawaken the bloodstained past. Of course, the Ustasi Croatian pro-Nazis would have to account for their actions, but prosecution of the leading Croatian Fascists was not always so simple. It was not until 1986 (at the exact moment when the Waldheim scandal broke), that the Minister of the Interior of the state of Croatia, the sinister Andrija Artuković was brought before the Zagreb courts, having found refuge in the United States for many years.[42]

The young Yugoslav state tried to find those initially responsible for the German occupation, but from 1948 onward the pressure was off. General Loehr was hanged in 1947, but his right-hand man, General Schmidt-Richberg, was released from prison before he had served the full term to which he had been sentenced after the war. Others avoided all punishment, either by escaping or by more radical means, such as the German commander-in-chief of the Zagreb district, General von Horstenau, who committed suicide during the surrender.

At the very moment when the Yugoslav War Crimes Commission was carefully compiling its files and transmitting them to London, the Yugoslav secret services in Vienna had very different preoccupations. They were trying to locate Austrians who had been compromised by Nazi extortion but only with the aim of evaluating how they could be turned, and forced into some sort of collaboration under the blessed protection of the silence which then prevailed in Austria.

Kurt Waldheim had not been a hero, nor was he an Eichmann. He belonged to that category which the Allied secret services called average people. Their wartime activities were not carefully examined. His stay in an American camp after the surrender had enabled him to evaluate the Allies' great capacity for closing their eyes.

Anton Kolendić, deputy director of the Yugoslav military delegation in Vienna from 1946 to 1948, and head of Yugoslav intelligence in that city, received a secret document in late 1947, sent to him from Belgrade. It contained a list of 30 war criminals living in Austria. Kurt Waldheim's name was on the list. The head of the diplomatic legation, Bogdan Kryzsman, was not informed, but Kolendić was thus well aware that this Foreign Ministry official to whom he paid daily visits had a far from clear conscience.

Four decades later, Anton Kolendić confirmed to us that he had passed this list on to his Soviet opposite number, Colonel Gonda. The latter commanded the Fourth District of Vienna, which was particularly interested by the Yugoslav list, because a number of the people mentioned on it lived in the zone under his control. The Yugoslav claims that he does not know what use the Soviets made of it, and it probably would have taken a long time to find out. The absolute silence observed by Moscow in 1986 when Kurt Waldheim was implicated clearly shows that the USSR, even less than the other three occupying powers in de-Nazified Austria insists on not recalling this period.

Yugoslavia and Austria are very close neighbors. During World War I, the Austro-Hungarian Empire mobilized its Croatian subjects, called superb soldiers by the Austrians, against the Serbs. Among the recruits to the 25th Infantry Regiment formed in Zagreb was a young man aged 21 named Josip Broz, who would later call himself "Tito". *Stabsfeldwebel* Broz, who at that time had a passion for the music of Johann Strauss, had always concealed his participation in the campaign which decimated 132,000 of the 250,000 Serbs who fought against the Emperor Franz-Josef's troops.

The Serbo-Croat conflict remained a terrible threat hanging over the federalist project of the Titoists.[43] Tito only broached it once more, under a cloak of secrecy, in 1941, to his companion-at-arms Aleksander Ranković, who was to become head of the Yugoslav secret police, the OZNA. On both sides of the Karawanken mountains which mark the Austro-Yugoslav frontier, the same reticence is shown about the past. Furthermore, it seems that Tito, even during his bitterest battles, retained a certain admiration for the German war machine. He thus discovered something of the spirit of chivalry when the *Abwehr* showed a desire to negotiate with him.

After 1945, the Yugoslav rulers lived in dread that the *modus vivendi* which the Four Great Powers had discovered in Vienna might crumble. They were haunted by a fear that Yugoslavia would be put through the mill of the "spheres of influence" strategy of East and West. "The entire struggle of the Yugoslav peoples was used as a bargaining counter between the great powers, even during the war," notes Vladimir Dedijer, Tito's principal biographer. Nor did events show his apprehensions to be unfounded. On September 21, 1944, Tito was in Stalin's office, where they met for the first time, when he learned of the British landing in Yugoslavia.

President Roosevelt did not hide his opposition to the territorial unity of Yugoslavia. In 1951, Winston Churchill revealed that an agreement had even been made between the USSR and Great Britain to split the country in half between them. One year later, Tito told his biographer, Dedijer, "The Russians did not inform us about the Yalta decisions although there were a genuine crime against Yugoslavia."[44] It was thus important for Belgrade to maintain the best possible relations with the new Austrian state and avoid any initiative that might destabilize it.

Not everyone in Yugoslavia shares this view of international relations, but history was on the move and was to violently shift the centers of interest of the young Republic. On March 18, 1948, exactly one month after the Allied Commission's decision to prosecute Kurt Waldheim, Stalin began to recall the Soviet experts who had been sent to Yugoslavia, on the pretext that Tito had criticized their extravagant lifestyle. Moscow was trying to wound its recalcitrant ally in its Achilles heel, economic recovery.

This gave the official ideologues the impetus to devise and emphasize political differences and differences of principle which made Tito a deviationist. Fearing a *coup d'etat*, Tito put under surveillance all those Yugoslav Communists who lent too sympathetic an ear to the anathemas pronounced by the Soviets. When the Kominform (the substitute for the defunct Communist International) officially issued sanctions against Yugoslavia on June 28, 1948, two internment camps for "Kominformists" were opened on two Yugoslavian islands in the Adriatic, Goli and Sveti-Grgur. OZNA secret policemen were thus mobilized for duties other than the pursuit of foreign nationals suspected of war crimes.

With the sudden deterioration in Soviet-Yugoslav

relations, the climate of uncertainty worsened in Belgrade. Fearing a military intervention, the Yugoslav rulers decided to evacuate the central archives, which contained much documentation about the war in the Balkans, even if the American forces had gotten hold of a lot of the Wehrmacht files at the time of the surrender.

During this transfer, documents were lost, or deliberately mislaid. The fratricidal battles within the resistance movement continued to cast a disturbing shadow over Yugoslav political life, and reconstruction also required silence in this case. Vladimir Dedijer, who had been made responsible for supervising these archives in 1947, managed to recover a few of them which he kept in his personal possession. When the central archives were restored to Belgrade, they were not subjected to systematic classification and analysis. The *Vecernje Novosti* journalists who were the first to discover the famous 1947 file against Kurt Waldheim claim that they unearthed it by the merest of chances. Furthermore, each of the Republics that make up the Yugoslav Federation jealously guards its own papers.

Up until 1954, the historic leaders of the resistance had retained a collective memory of the black years. Certainly, the OZNA had concentrated on seeking out German soldiers who might have been involved in unfortunate episodes for the Communist power. The secret police thus managed to eliminate all the German protagonists in those mysterious negotiations between the Abwher and the partisans in March, 1943. Siegfried Kasche, Minister Plenipotentiary of the Third Reich in Zagreb, was condemned to death and hanged after a trial which was held in the greatest secrecy. General von Horstenau committed suicide, but the third man in the affair, Hans Ott, managed to flee to Austria. An OZNA team had no hesitation in going over there to kidnap him; they brought him back to Yugoslavia, grilled him and summarily liquidated him.

It would have been much more difficult to apply such expeditious methods to a senior official attached to the office of the head of the Austrian diplomatic corps, especially as the stakes were not comparable. According to Tito's own son, Misha Broz, the Yugoslav ruler must have known all about Kurt Waldheim's compromising past, but he considered his case to be insignificant.

Broz junior, a solid businessman who calmly admits that he does not hold a Yugoslav Communist League card, provided these details to a special correspondent of the *Jerusalem Post* in June, 1986, on the island of Brioni where his job was to host the conference of OPEC ministers, who were meeting at this vacation resort of which Tito had been so fond.[45] Former Yugoslav Vice-president Mitja Ribicić considers that Marshall Tito knew and that he tried to profit by it with Waldheim, who had become UN Secretary-General.

Tito's opinion of Kurt Waldheim was not shared unanimously in Yugoslav ruling circles, but from 1954 onward, many of his former companions-at-arms had themselves become targets. This purge arranged by a man who had previously sworn that "our revolution will not devour its children" was unleashed by the eviction of another leading figure in the Yugoslav resistance movement, Milovan Djilas. Denouncing the bureaucracy, and the pseudo-aristocratic airs affected by the fighters in the shadows who now basked in the glory of power, Djilas was isolated and sent to prison on two occasions. Vladimir Dedijer was expelled from the Party in 1955 for having defended him. Eleven years later, for very different reasons, Rankovcić, the main organizer of Tito's political police was himself fingered. He was even accused of having tapped the illustrious Marshall's own phone, in his coplike mania.

The Yugoslav state which watched Kurt Waldheim preside over the United Nations in 1972 was thus not really the same post-war Yugoslavia. The only veteran who agreed to comment on the Waldheim affair in 1986, Vladimir Dedijer, stated, "I had known Tito since 1937, I fought with him against the Nazis, I confronted Stalin with him. Yet after 1954, our relationship was much less close. By 1972, Tito was already very old. Perhaps they didn't look for him in the archives."

In the Service of an Amnesiac State

VIENNA was called liberated but not from its new occupiers who remained until 1955, and not from its history which it avoided like the plague. More than the plague, in fact, because a there is a monument to the plague on the Graben, while the memory of the 65,000 Viennese Jews who were the victims of Nazism is not perpetuated in any monument.

"A Russian soldier in a fur cap goes by with a rifle over his shoulder, a few tarts cluster round the American Information Office and men in overcoats sip ersatz coffee in the windows of the Old Vienna," writes Graham Greene in *The Third Man*[46]. In Vienna, the postwar austerity had assumed the air of self-punishment, morbidly emphasizing that the "fin-de-siècle" graces were over forever.

Europe was reconstructed without following the plans cynically drawn up by Churchill and Stalin in 1944. When the Cold War began to take shape, the Allied War Crimes Commission was dissolved, leaving undone no less than 36,000 prosecutions against suspects. A list of these 36,000 names was actually sent to the member countries. With the exception of a few Nazi-hunters and the Israeli police, the pursuit of war criminals was abandoned.

Austria was not a member of the Commission and thus did not receive this list of 36,000 people who had been absolved by default, pardoned by lassitude. In any case, Austria would not have done anything with it. Collectively stamped as victims of Nazism, the Austrians wanted more than anyone else, to turn over a new leaf. In the confidential resumé which Kurt Waldheim submitted to Fritz Molden in 1945, his war years in the Balkans are explicitly recalled, for the last time until 1986. Yet his secret was well kept.

When Kurt Waldheim embarked upon his ascent up the ladder of the Ministry of Foreign Affairs, the situation could be summarized as follows: the Secret Services (Western, Soviet and Yugoslav) knew but said nothing; the politicians did not want to know and said even less.

The traces of a conspiracy lurk within this persistent ambiguity. Kurt Waldheim might have been involved in the enigmatic Nazi International which at the fall of the Third Reich, had ordered its members to infiltrate the machinery of state and occupy important positions while awaiting better days. This theory has been put forward but it does not fit in with Kurt Waldheim's personality, which led him to become involved in the Nazi machine by chance rather than by conviction.

One might also wonder whether the young Austrian civil servant had become a double, triple, or even quadruple agent, in order to pay the price of absolution. His behavior during the Prague Spring seems to support this hypothesis. He was then head of the Austrian diplomatic corps, and he ordered the Austrian Embassy in the Czechoslovakian capital which had been invaded by Soviet tanks in April 1968 to close its doors to any political refugee. The ambassador at the time was Rudolf Kirschläger, who later became President of Austria and whom Waldheim succeeded on June 8, 1986. He was so disgusted by these orders that he refused to obey them.

Rather than an obscure machination, this incident reveals above all the opportunism which is so characteristic of Waldheim, this capacity to follow the turn of events rather than to make history. The former Oberleutnant did not need to be the agent of a foreign power in order to act in this way. It was sufficient that he was a devoted agent of the new Austrian state which, by accepting him as one of its servants, had dispensed with the slightest need for him to account in the least for his past.

The theory representing Kurt Waldheim as the Machiavellian agent of the superpowers is actually rather reassuring, although it cannot be proved. It allows one to consider the post-war world without the formidable duplicity which is so characteristic of it. Behind the international consensus that "never again" shall Nazism triumph, there lay the most selfish calculations, the most implacable reasons of state. In 1985, for instance, it was discovered that the Vice-Chairman of an international commission of the UN—one which was by no means insignificant, the Commission on Human Rights—the East German Hermann Klenner, had been a Nazi Party activist. The revelation shocked very few people.

One year later, after Kurt Waldheim's electoral success and its tacit approval by the Western capitals, even those who created and ran the United Nations recognized that the principles of the institution are invalidated. A minor Austrian official, by crawling up the ladder of power on all fours, has severely rocked the foundations of this Tower of Babel of modern times.

4

The Silence of the Nations

The busy day works
Far away in confused noises
And through the meaningless din of voices
I discern the blows of heavy hammers.

Schiller

AFTER his failure to win the Austrian Presidency in 1971, Kurt Waldheim's career seemed to be at a dead end. The electoral defeat of the People's Party in October, 1970 had ended in the etablishment of a one-party Socialist government led by Chancellor Kreisky. Kurt Waldheim, who was then aged 52, had been in charge of the Ministry of Foreign Affairs for two years, and now found himself in an awkward position. Should he return to diplomacy? It would be hard to see how he could take orders from those who had formerly been taking orders from him. Should he become more deeply involved in politics? The bitter defeat he had suffered when he ran against the Socialist Franz Jonas did not put him in a position to rally the conservative forces which had been defeated by the new strong man of Austria, Bruno Kreisky, another veteran of the Ballhausplatz, the address of the Austrian Ministry of Foreign Affairs.

Kurt Waldheim owes the solution to his problem to the new chancellor. Kreisky knew Waldheim well. Waldheim had been one of his underlings throughout Kreisky's long career as Secretary of State, then Minister of Foreign Affairs. He received Kurt Waldheim's reports as an ambassador, first from Ottawa, then from New York. "They were the dullest and most insipid reports I ever read," the retired chancellor now admits.

Yet until the revelations about Kurt Waldheim's past became sufficiently overwhelming for him to be forced to distance himself from Waldheim, Bruno Kreisky always spoke of "my friend, Kurt Waldheim". This was more of a strategic than a genuine friendship, for the two men have nothing in common, neither political convictions, life history, nor lifestyle. Nevertheless, Bruno Kreisky felt that the man would be useful to him. He was sufficiently familiar with the world to know that a diplomat of Waldheim's type, with neither the personality nor the ability to make his personal mark, can sometimes prove to be more useful than a Metternich, especially when one is representing a small country of negligible importance on the world scene.

UN Secretary General

THE renewal of the UN Secretary-General's term of office came at just the right moment to solve Kurt Waldheim's career problem. U Thant's mandate had expired, and a successor had to be found.

The two Superpowers were in détente at the time—it was the beginning of the major negotiations between the two Germanies and the start of the long and difficult search for a solution to the Vietnamese conflict. They did not want to have to tackle the question of finding a new Secretary-General. The USA and the USSR would far rather have had U Thant seek a third term in office, but he was ill and absolutely refused to do so. So each side proposed its own candidate. The Soviets were in favor of a Swede, Gunnar Jarring, a former ambassador to Moscow. The Americans supported a Finn, Max Jakobson, his country's ambassador to the United Nations. Yet each of them came up against the veto of the country which had not chosen them.

Max Jakobson, back in business in Helsinki, explained to us why the Soviets vetoed his election. "'Our Arab friends would never have agreed to vote for a Jew as UN Secretary-General,' I was told by the Soviet delegates to the United Nations." But Max Jakobson does not consider this to be the main reason for his defeat. "My concept of the role of the Secretary-General displeased everyone, in fact. I was in favor of stronger powers for him and a more interventionist attitude when a crisis arose."

Bruno Kreisky's proposal of Kurt Waldheim as a

compromise candidate was thus most fortuitous. For the West, as well as for the Soviets, Austria was the symbol of the policy of détente between East and West. The Austrian State Treaty of 1955 which guaranteed the unity and neturality of the country marked an end to the acute phase of the cold war. Furthermore, this man was well-known in the glass building by the East River. The past 10 years he spent as head of the Austrian delegation to the United Nations made his tall silhouette a familiar sight. And above all, he didn't frighten anyone.

The American ambassador, Seymour Maxwell Finger, who was assistant to George Bush when he headed the US delegation to the United Nations admits that "no one saw him as a man of principle. We believed him to be an opportunist, but in the 1970's we wanted a Secretary-General who would be malleable. We had one for ten years." When the vote was taken in the Security Council (which preceded the vote taken on December 22, 1971 in the General Assembly) of all the Western nations, only Great Britain abstained. The reasons why remain obscure and have never been the subject of a detailed explanation.

Of course, the key question remains. Did the great powers elect Kurt Waldheim in the full knowledge of his past? For Seymour Maxwell Finger, the American delegation were satisfied with the resumé which Kurt Waldheim submitted to the American Mission, giving the expurgated version of his military record. The Yugoslavs, who had actually compiled the file on Kurt Waldheim which is preserved in the UN War Crimes Commission archives, made no objection to his promotion. From 1958 onward, Tito had ordered his services not to take issue with the ambitious diplomat. It seems that on all sides, people were only too happy to have found the right man for anyone to start an ill-considered investigation which might endanger such a convenient solution to the problem.

Only China opposed his election at first, not out of defiance but because it wanted a Secretary-General from the Third World. As soon as he was elected, Kurt Waldheim hastened to Peking to erase this bad impression, and received a royal welcome. Yet he still did not receive Chinese support for his election to a third term as head of the United Nations.

No matter what, on December 22, 1971 the Austrian diplomat was chosen to occupy the thirty-eighth floor of UN headquarters in New York for the next ten years—because his mandate was renewed in 1976. Kurt Waldheim himself knew what was at stake. If there were a scandal, his whole beloved career would be ruined. "Before he went any further," says a UN official, "he made sure that the American and Soviet representatives, who customarily hold prior consultations, were unaware of his past or had decided to forget it."

It should be said that his cover was very successful. Thirteen years later, Julia Bright a journalist on the London *Sunday Times* who had excellent contacts at the United Nations and who didn't much care for Kurt Waldheim, was still taken in by the mendacious biography that he had submitted when he acceded to office. In any event, Kurt Waldheim was playing a very dangerous game, and if in his autobiography he claims to have been strolling calmly in Central Park while awaiting the result of the debate in the Security Council, he must certainly have been prey to a moment of deep emotion on that day.

"No country could doubt Kurt Waldheim's suitability," recalls Kosciusko-Morizet, the French representative on the Security Council at the time of the vote in question. "Some people found him rather dreary, but he had no serious opponent. Personally, I had received the order from my minister, Maurice Schumann, to vote for him. If any inquiry into his past had been held at the time, I was never made aware of it." Arkadi Shevchenko, the Soviet Deputy Secretary-

General of the United Nations, who defected to the West while Waldheim was running the international organization, confirms for his part, "No one in Moscow was interested in what he was doing as a young man, and no one dug into his biography. The Yugoslavs would certainly have told the Soviets about his past in the German army, but the Soviets are worse record-keepers than the Americans. The information was probably lost in some bureaucratic files, and no one cared." (*New York Times*, June 15, 1986)

A senior UN official told the authors, "An odorless, colorless diplomat was required, and the criteria for the choice were specific. For instance, France preferred Waldheim to Jakobson because the former spoke French and the latter did not." Yet again, his knowledge of languages had settled his future.

Of all the powers involved, the United States seemed to be the most likely to have had useful information about Kurt Waldheim. The former American Ambassador to the United Nations, Daniel Patrick Moynihan, thus noted in a book of memoirs published in 1978, that he once told George Bush, "Our candidate [Jakobson] was a Socialist Jew but instead we installed a German infantry officer."

The Israeli Absolution

THERE was just one country which might have shown greater vigilance than the others; that country was Israel. Yet the Jewish state, whether by calculation, naivety, or political opportunism, had high hopes of Waldheim's election to the head of United Natons. It was hoped that he would lend a less willing ear than his predecessor to the theories of the enemies of the Jewish State. Above all, it was hoped he would foster the emigration of Soviet Jews. Vienna had become the stopover point for this, thanks to Chancellor Kreisky. It was thus not considered in good taste in Tel Aviv to voice doubts about the past and the moral values of a man of whom so much might be expected.

The first journalist to have questioned Kurt Waldheim about his Nazi past, fifteen years ago, was Haim Yavin. This was a bitter experience. As Director of Israeli Television in 1986, he explained to the authors how as a very young correspondent in New York, he had requested an interview with Kurt Waldheim on the very day of his election. "A member of the Austrian delegation whispered in my ear that he had had a Nazi past. Nothing definite. This information was new to me. So I asked him, 'Did you have any links with the Nazi party? Were you a party member?' He seemed rather embarrassed, but I was quite nervous myself; in any case he didn't start sweating. On the contrary, he put on a big smile, shook his head, and told me, 'No links of any sort. On the contrary, my family had a lot of problems during the Nazi period. My father was an official and a resolute anti-Nazi, as we all were, my brother and sister as well. My father was fired from his teaching post and thrown in jail. So you can be certain that there was no reason to cherish the least friendly sentiment toward the Nazis. On the contrary, we suffered under their domination.'"

Yavin moved on to other questions. "'When did you hear about the Holocaust and what had been done to the Jews?'—'Well, I had Jewish friends when I was in high school. Some of them live in New York and have been in touch with me. I was deeply moved when I heard about that sort of thing and couldn't believe it. But there was not much we could do.'"

Without denying that he wore a Wehrmacht lieutenant's uniform on the Russian front, Kurt Waldheim admitted that he had been wounded in 1941. "The good Lord helped me and I was sent back home to resume my studies." He also stated that when Austria was occupied by the Nazis, in 1938, no country lifted a finger to help it. "The people who criticize us today ought to remember the call for help to Austria at the time of the Anschluss."

With the satisfaction of work well done, Haim Yavin sent back his four-minute interview. It was broadcast. Then, "I felt as though the sky had fallen in on me and that I had done something terrible. The broadcasting authorities and the newspapers were furious with me for having dared to put such unpleasant questions to such a friendly man." *Davar* (Labor) and *Haaretz* (Independent) were two newspapers that considered the interview to be impertinent. The *Jerusalem Post* judged Yavin to have interrogated Waldheim "in an aggressive tone." The Foreign Ministry reacted with ill humor, "I was told that my interview might anger an important Austrian leader, such as Waldheim, when we needed to have good relations with that country, at a time when an increasing exodus of Soviet Jews were passing through Vienna."

A Skullcap and Strudels

ANDRÉ Lewin who was Waldheim's press secretary and the French translator of his writing remembers the warm welcome the Israeli leaders gave Secretary-General Waldheim. "Golda Meir invited him home and cooked for him. No one made any mention of his past."

And why would the Jews refuse to deal with him? He seemed to have world credibility. Didn't he boast to having received a miniature tool kit from George Bush as a Christmas gift in 1972? Didn't he tell how he and his wife ate caviar for breakfast during his official visit to Moscow? Did he not delight in counting the number of gun salutes which greeted his visit to African potentates? In his euphoric state at all these honors—after all, he had begun his career at the UN in 1955 as a mere observer—Kurt Waldheim could only rejoice at Israel's responsible attitude.

Israel belived that it had gained from the deal, Waldheim being far more desirable than his predecessors U Thant and Dag Hammarskjöld. There were only a few shadows cast over this relatively harmonious picture. In July 1976, Kurt Waldheim blundered over the Israeli raid on Entebbe, calling it, "A serious violation of Ugandan sovereignty." Israel rebuked him. Waldheim then stated that he was satisfied with the fact that the operation had enabled 104 lives to be saved.

The former permanent representative of Israel at the United Nations, Yehuda Blum, injects some spite into the picture he paints of Kurt Waldheim. Yet it was well-known that the two men were on excellent terms in the reception rooms and corridors of the UN Waldheim mentions him in the latest rehash of his autobiography as being "a nice man who speaks German."

Yehuda Blum concedes that during a recent stay in Vienna—before the affair broke—he telephoned Waldheim and invited him to lunch. "I still ask myself how such an uninteresting man could have reached such a position. He gives me the impression of a little politician. I never managed to talk to him about anything but politics," says Blum who claims to have been unaware of his Nazi past and even the existence of the United Nations files on Nazi criminals. "I am sure that no one in the Israeli delegation knew about it." Yet, Gideon Raphael who was Israeli Ambassador to the United Nations from 1967–1968, having been a member of the Israeli delegation from the creation of the State of Israel until 1953, confirms that he himself was well aware of the existence of such archives. As for Kurt Waldheim, he knew him when Waldheim was still Austrian Ambassador to the United Nations, and he describes him as "a superficial human being whose principal gift was for making political evaluations which were invariably wrong."

However, the strangest episode and the biggest *faux pas* occured during the 31 hour visit which Kurt Waldheim paid to Israel on July 30 and 31, 1973. Shortly after his arrival, he was taken to Yad Vashem, the Holocaust memorial, in Jerusalem. Gideon Hausner, former prosecutor at the Eichmann trial, guided him through the museum, showing him the photographs of the genocide of the Jews, and stopping for a long time before a large reproduction of Mauthausen, the Austrian concentration camp. Hausner says that Kurt Waldheim listened to him carefully, and replied three or four times, "Yes, yes, I know," or "I remember it," when he passed in front of pictures illustrating the Anschluss.

They then went toward the *Ohel Yizkor,* which literally means 'Tent of Remembrance.' An eternal flame burns in the semi-darkness, in memory of the six million Jews who were victims of the Holocaust. The names of the concentration camps are engraved on black tablets. This is a place of prayer. A guard handed Kurt Waldheim a skullcap for him to cover his head before entering. He refused to take it and entered the crypt. Yad Vashem's director, Haim Pazner, ran after him to offer him another skullcap. Waldheim took it and put it in his pocket. Hausner tried to persuade him to put it on. Waldheim said no. "I decided not to interrupt the ceremony, but the fact is that Waldheim was the first visitor to Yad Vashem ever to have refused to cover his head during this ceremony," Hausner recalls.

To explain his refusal, Waldheim says, "I came here as Secretary-General of the United Nations and in my own way, I honor the Jewish people who have suffered so much." The incident caused a scandal. Kurt Waldheim's visit was spoiled by it. On the next day, he tried to make honorable amends by agreeing to put a white skullcap on his head to visit a synagogue. That evening, he committed another *faux pas.*

The Minister of Foreign Affairs, Abba Eban, gave a dinner in his honor at his residence in Jerusalem. "I made a toast to him. He replied that he saluted Jerusalem, our magnificent capital. Did he do so deliberately? It's still an open question," Eban says today. Such an expression could have enraged the Arabs. The conquest of the eastern part of Jerusalem, and its annexation, followed by the official proclamation of the eternal capital of the Jewish state have never been acknowledged by them, or indeed by the rest of the international community. Tel Aviv is Israel's capital city.

As usual, Kurt Waldheim hastened to publish an elaborate communiqué which stated, "that he used this conventional expression inadvertently as an impromptu response to a toast. The United Nations position on the status of Jerusalem is well known and it was evidently not my intention to disassociate myself from it." Kurt Waldheim returned to Jerusalem four years later. The Director of the Israeli Ministry of Foreign Affairs, Shlomo Avinery, gave a lecture at the Hebrew University on Mount Scopus on February 10, 1977, on relations between Austria and Israel, in Waldheim's presence. "As you know, Mr. Waldheim, the Austrian Emperor once held the title of King of Jerusalem," said Avinery, with flattery which he now regrets. Kurt Waldheim replied that he was deeply moved to find himself there once again. "And I must also thank you for your wonderful apple strudel which seems to me to taste even better than in Vienna."

The Tail of the Russian Bear

KURT Waldheim would later claim to have been the victim of slanders about his past due to his impartial attitude in the Middle Eastern conflict. This is a very treacherous explanation. It suggests the existence of a Jewish-Israeli plot.

Nor does it correspond to reality, since when faced with the Israel-Arab confrontation, as with all the other great international upheavals, the UN Secretary-General made it his job to do exactly what the great powers wanted.

Ever since it was created in 1945, the United Nations Organization has been under the control of Moscow and Washington, who shared the same repugnance for an international forum in which all the votes have similar weight. The UN Secretary-General would thus have to try and take into account the Third World's aspirations without ever upsetting the equilibrium of the world as defined by the two superpowers.

Kurt Waldheim was more inclined to play this game than anyone else. When, for instance, the head of the PLO, Yasser Arafat, caused a sensation by mounting the UN rostrum on November 3, 1974, the Austrian diplomat was careful to place the responsibility for this incident on the President of the General Assembly, Algerian Abdelaziz Bouteflika. His natural caution was reinforced by the scandal created around the revolver holster which the Palestinian leader ostentatiously wore on his belt.

"On the political level, Kurt Waldheim did not particularly favor the Soviet Union during his two terms of office. He was above all a careerist who was ready to do anything to take care of his future." This observation made by a senior UN official is of itself a reply to those fertile imaginations who have cherished the idea that the former *Oberleutnant* had been a zealous Soviet agent during his six years at the head of the United Nations. "This organization is a glasshouse, and those who know it well can only burst out laughing at the theory that Kurt Waldheim could maintain an attitude of impartiality while at the same time being able to secretly communicate vital information to this or that government," writes a shrewd American observer of the UN scene.[47]

As for Arkadi Shevchenko, who shows no particular gratitude to Waldheim for he did not prove to be particularly cooperative when Shevchenko defected to the West, he confirms in the interview already mentioned, "The USSR never tried to make Waldheim talk. No one, not even the KGB, ever said to me, 'Arkady, you can help us get our people into the UN because we have compromising information on Waldheim.'" One of his former collaborators concluded, "It was useless to try and make Waldheim talk. He talked enough without any prompting."

True, the Austrian diplomat had always displayed a great fascination for the Soviet Union. In post-war Vienna, the Soviets first arrived as the masters, unilaterally recognizing the provisional government of the Socialist Renner, who had once been a convinced supporter of the Anschluss. Harry Truman and Winston Churchill had to intercede with Stalin for the Western allies to be able to share the Viennese cake.

Kurt Waldheim ostensibly approved of Chancellor Raab, who once said that it was "useless to spend our time twisting the tail of the Russian bear." As a great admirer of Nikita Khrushchev, he was delighted to be placed on the left of Jakob Malik, the Soviet delegate to the United Nations, during an official luncheon shortly before he was elected Secretary-General. After the Soviet invasion of Afghanistan on December 27, 1979, he was reproached for his lack of haste in condemning this violation of international law.

A less well-known incident caused certain people in the West to suspect him of collusion with Moscow when in fact, he revealed his disdain for anything not done by the book. In spring 1978, Kurt Waldheim signed the nomination of a Soviet official, Geli Dneprovsky, for the ultra-sensitive post of Director of Personnel at UN headquarters in Europe. He thus handed over the supervision of 3,000 employees of international organizations to a man whom the American and

British intelligence services accused of being a KGB colonel. The Secretary-General apologized obsequiously, ordered an investigation into Dneprovsky, and buried the matter.

If the Soviet Union holds an important place in the preoccupations of the Austrian diplomat, he is nevertheless well aware that the UN would be nothing without the financial support given to it by the United States. The United Nations cannot exist without its American subsidies, which enable it to maintain its gigantic activity—the reports produced each year cover a thousand million pages and it organizes about 7,000 international meetings a year. In 1984, a financial report indicated that the budgetary deficit of the organization had reached 166 million dollars, and 90 of the member countries were only paying an infinitesimal proportion of their dues. Of the delinquent payers, the USSR was outstanding by being 42.5 million dollars in arrears, and this power was even seeking to pay part of its share in non-convertible rubles.

The Decline of the United Nations

KURT Waldheim's rule corresponds, in fact, to the organizational and political decline of the United Nations. This has been a long process, which would culminate in the American and British boycott of UNESCO in 1985. Kurt Waldheim certainly did not provoke this, but he was part of the problem. "He was an appalling administrator," notes a UN expert, "At the very moment when the organization most needed austerity and rationalization."

Each of Kurt Waldheim's predecessors played a specific role, politically conversial but crucial. The Norwegian Trygve Lie had accompanied the first steps of the organization through the pitfalls of the postwar era and the cold war. His successor, Dag Hammarsköld, met with a tragic fate (his death in the former Belgian Congo during the upheavals that followed that country's independence remains a mystery) for having wanted to turn the organization and its Secretary-General into a power capable of intervention and decision which could restrain the superpowers. The Burmese U Thant in his two terms of office worked effectively to bring the stream of countries which had gained independence in the 1960's into the family of nations.

Each of these three men prove in their own way that the personal actions of a UN Secretary-General can sometimes be decisive and that his historic merits cannot be measured by the yardstick of how scrupulous he is in sticking to the minutiae of the rules of the organization. They prove wrong the denigrators of this contraption, as General de Gaulle called the United Nations of which he was so contemptuous.

For all its faults, its bureaucracy, its appearance of impotence when confronted with the superpowers, its ridiculous resolutions passed under the pressure of automatic majorities, this sometimes noisy forum in which each country, however small, has the right to speak, is useful, even if only sporadically, through the intervention of its peace-keeping forces, the blue berets, who create a semblance of peace and security.

Even if his predecessors gave some credibility to this view, the same cannot be said of Kurt Waldheim's ten-year presence at the head of the UN. The confidence of the whole word on which he insisted at the beginning of his 1986 electoral campaign was more of the type one gives to a well-trained valet. All the direct witnesses to his activities whom the authors were able to interview agreed in their judgements of his character. "Dull, conceited, hard on his subordinates, obsequious with the powerful," seems to be picture of the man to whom no one would ever have dreamed of attributing the malice of a major criminal.

"Of my meetings with him," says Abba Eban, the former Israeli Minister of Foreign Affairs, "I have retained the impression that this man is living proof of the untruth of the dictum that nature abhors a vacuum. He is vacuum itself. Neuter and neutral. The opposite of an exceptional human being. He was ideal for the job of U N Secretary-General where no intellectual initiative is required." For Max Jakobson, he represents, "The essence of the German bureaucrat, diligent and unimaginative." He is credited with only one attempt, which was swiftly aborted, at trying to impose his views on the international community. In 1972, after the massacre of the Israeli athletes by Palestinian commandos during the Munich Olympic Games, West German Chancellor Willy Brandt asked the UN Secretary General to use his powers to place the question of terrorism on the agenda of the General Assembly. Kurt Waldheim acceded to this request, but soon retracted when faced with the opposition of the Arab countries and the Soviet bloc. It was not until 1985 that the subject once again headed the agenda. But Kurt Waldheim was no longer there.

"He had an enormous ego," says Seymour Maxwell Finger. "He wanted to be recognized as a world leader. At the same time, he had this caution which enabled him to accede to the wishes of the powerful. This contradiction between his ambition and his caution made him a frustrated and dissatisfied man."

Portrait of a Lover of Power

ONE of his closest colleagues, a man who still works at the United Nations (and who, for this reason, has asked to remain anonymous) was doubtless a victim of this frustration. In fact, he remembers the methods which Kurt Waldheim used to impose his authority on his staff: "It was usually when I had managed to get a seat at the opera that he would keep me at the office until late in the evening for trivia. No ambassador waited for less than 40 minutes before entering his office. This is how he avenged himself, even if his work schedule did not require it, for having been himself kept waiting in the past."

"The whole world has known Mr. Waldheim since 1972, and I can assure you that he behaved like a creep in the United Nations' glass palace on the East River in New York. My God, how can I explain it? The man was like a sort of obsequious maitre d', who could bend backward and forward at the same time. Certainly, he was a hard worker, that's undeniable, but did the Emperor Franz-Josef himself spend his whole life with his nose in his paperwork? Has he ever had anything else to than 'That's very good, I liked that very much.'?"

"There is even a rumor that he had his apples peeled for him, but that's just a story. In any case, it fits him nicely. He is basically a Feudalist. He is amazingly generous with other people's resources. Mind you, that's not so silly because it allows him to wield all the machinery of diplomacy in order to get his toilet paper sent by pouch to London from New York. Don't laugh, it's true! The Waldheim family considered that the Americans made a better quality product than the Austrians. It may be true but tell me, couldn't he have had it mailed like everyone else?

"Recent events have proved that Mr. Waldheim's memory was defective as far as his war years were concerned. He also 'forgot' to remit to the UN all the gifts he had been given in his official capacity, as is the custom. Appropriating the gifts is certainly not illegal but it is considered inappropriate. Mr. Waldheim has not the least idea of what is or is not the correct thing to do, as far as this is concerned. For instance, the President of Mexico presented him with a very valuable old clock, which Waldheim arranged to have sent to his home beside Lake Atter, near Salzburg. He had the cheek to have the transportation costs paid for by the UN. This may seem petty, but you've no idea the harm it does to the United Nations' image.

"When Mr. Waldheim traveled to Teheran to try and mediate in the American hostage affair, he was not received by the Ayatollah Khomeini. The reason for this was not solely a political one. The Shah had once given Waldheim some diamonds which he kept for himself. Khomeini is not the kind of man to forgive that kind of thing. In this respect, I should add that Waldheim does not understand anything about revolutions. The crowds of men in open-necked shirts who come and go in the gilded halls of overthrown monarchs make him feel ill at ease, and what's more they don't give a damn about protocol.

"Waldheim is always very meticulous about protocol. He likes to have the red carpet rolled out for him, he likes salvos fired in his honor and being awarded decorations. He is also very comfortable at hosting receptions, choosing the dishes and the wines with something like emotion. Politics interests him far less. He doesn't understand much about it anyway. In his autobiography, he explains how he reached the conclusion that personalities have a greater influence on the destiny of the world than any other factor. On the basis of this conviction, as soon as he became Secretary-General of the UN, he spent his time visiting as many heads of state as possible, preferably in Africa, less willingly in Western Europe, because there the Secretary-General of the United Nations is received like any Minister of Foreign Affairs. Not so in Africa. The humblest UN official is received there like a king. Mr. Waldheim returned full of enthusiasm from each of his trips to Africa. Naturally, it would never have occurred to him to leave these official receptions to sit, if only for a second, beside the victims of the drought in the Sahel.[48]

"In the same way, he has never bothered to go down and visit the lower floors of UN headquarters where the clerks work. He had one of the building's six elevators reserved for his exclusive use, which caused the most terrible over-crowding at peak hours. Minor details, you think? Maybe, but they'll give you some idea of what he's like. This may have nothing to do with your concerns about him, but you should know that he never reads a book, and he knows as much about culture as my basset-hound.

"Just as disgraceful is the way his daughter, Lieselotte, has had such a swiftly-moving career in the United Nations. You ought to know that anyone who got in the way of this lady was quickly put in his place by her father. Several of the most brilliant senior UN officials have discovered how dangerous it was to attack the Waldheims. Perhaps this is part of their sense of family and the Christian values on which they pride themselves.

"Lieselotte is now head of protocol at the United Nations in Geneva. That job fits a Waldheim like a glove. A feeling for representation seems to be hereditary in this family. Mr. Waldheim has always been a representative. He has never governed. He has been the most expensive postman of all time. He's always traveling, always visiting the great people of this world. Those who have impressed him have been the tallest of the great ones, as one can tell by reading his autobiography. The Syrian President Hafez Al-Assad, for instance, 'whose height and rugged face are impressive.' El-Zayyat, the former Egyptian Minister of Foreign Affairs is 'tall and well-built.' Sekou Touré is also, 'a tall, good-looking, even an imposing man.' Finally, Saddam Hussein, now President of Iraq, he describes as 'very big, looking like a heavyweight boxer.' Anyone not fortunate enough to be tall enough to look Mr. Waldheim directly in the eye—King Hussein of Jordan, for instance—had no right to that kind of compliment.

"Ridiculous, isn't it? True, but those are the things that really matter to Mr. Waldheim. As proof, when he was still Austrian Minister of Foreign Affairs, he wanted at all costs to restrict entry into the diplomatic corps to very tall people. He found the round, chubby type too inelegant, not imposing enough. In the thousand-year Reich there was also a predilection for tall, slim figures. But that's not what I'm trying to say.

"One of my colleagues told me one day that Waldheim was a 'man without qualities.' He had no smell, no taste, no feelings. I disagree. Mr. Waldheim can get very enthusiastic. Especially about himself. I've never met anyone as arrogant in my whole life. When he became UN Secretary-General he moved into a three-story house on Sutton Place. Naturally, this is one of the most fashionable addresses in Manhattan. This mansion, a bequest from Arthur A. Houghton, Jr., President and CEO of the Steuben Glass Company, was furnished at UN expense. Mrs. Waldheim insisted upon Louis XV sofas, Saxe porcelain and English lace. The Metropolitan Museum of Art was among those invited to hang a few Corots and Gainsboroughs in the reception rooms.

"It could, of course, be claimed that to some extent luxurious accommodations befit the status of a UN Secretary-General. But I would reply that Waldheim's predecessors were satisfied, without any harm being done to the job, with much more modest lifestyles. Dag Hammarskjöld made do with a small apartment, and U Thant stayed in Riverdale in an ordinary neighborhood. It would never have occurred to them to make the UN pay for ordinary household items like bed linen, towels or laundry detergent. You don't believe me? The Director of Finance at the United Nations still blushes with shame when he is reminded of it.

"There's no need to worry about Mr. Waldheim's financial situation, even though he told an Austrian newspaper that he had never been able to save any money when he was UN Secretary-General. One could go on forever wondering how Kurt Waldheim could have spent his money. There's not a waiter in a New York café who ever saw him leave a single penny as a tip. His country house beside Lake Atter ought not to have made a big hole in his budget. The land only cost him about 7 dollars a square yard, although ordinary mortals pay prices that are several dozen times higher for land in the same area. Today, he gets an annual pension of 83,000 dollars, as a former UN Secretary-General and a former diplomat of the Austrian Ministry of Foreign Affairs. Tax-free, of course."

5
An Interplay of Rumor and Chance

A blood-red ray spreads over the ground,
it is a little light filtering under the door.
Now it is being opened. . . .

Sacher-Masoch

Is chance a factor in the making of history? Candidates for a master's dissertation in philosophy who decide to expound on this subject are no longer reduced to using the examples of Cleopatra's nose or Isaac Newton's apple. Chance would one day have to catch up with a man who had spent his life erasing its effects. It was at the very moment that he had climbed the last rung of the ladder he had so patiently constructed and which appeared to be solid enough to take any strain that the incident occurred.

Who would have believed that in the month of September, 1985, when Kurt Waldheim was officially contending for the highest office in his land, that the fiercest controversy in post-war Austria would develop? The time corresponded to the rising power of the Conservative opposition. People were tired of the Socialist government, in power for 15 years. Although Kurt Waldheim was not an official member of the People's Party, he was the natural standard-bearer for the Conservatives. His experience as UN Secretary-General made him the world's best-known Austrian after Chancellor Kreisky. The latter refused to come out of retirement to try and save the presidency, which had been a Socialist monopoly for the SPÖ since 1945. "I want to save the country the cost of a state funeral," Kreisky argued to justify his refusal.

The Socialists did not have high hopes when they chose the former Minister of Health, Dr. Kurt Steyrer to run against Kurt Waldheim. He was certainly a likeable man, warm-hearted and approachable in a small group, but he was a mediocre speaker, totally lacking in charisma, and suffering from a lack of credibility because of his fluctuation over the thorny problem of the construction of a power station at Hainburg, which the Ecology Party violently opposed.

It was at this point that a rumor began to spread through Vienna that Kurt Waldheim's past was not as pure as the biographies freely distributed through the federal press service had people believe. From the Landtmann café to Leopold Hawelka's bar, via the Oswald und Kalb restaurant, the traditional meeting places of Viennese journalists and politicians, there was talk, at first in whispers but growing louder, about Waldheim's situation.

The Shadow of General Loehr

THE originator of the rumors was a certain Georg Tidl, a historian and Socialist Party member who worked occasionally with Austrian television. He was interested in the story of General Loehr who had been condemned to death for war crimes and shot by the Yugoslavs in 1947. The reason why this character preoccupied him is because Loehr's daughter (who had often declared that her father had been an innocent victim of the war) was trying to get a commemorative plaque fixed to the house in Vienna where he lived. A ceremony had even been arranged for the purpose, during which Defense Minister Friedhelm Frischenschlager, the same who had heaped honors on the returning war criminal Walter Reder when he came home from prison in Italy, was to solemnly unveil the plaque. The feelings this aroused in left-wing and intellectual circles caused Georg Tidl to delve deep into the Balkan war archives.

Quite accidentally, and without seeking any particular angle, he discovered the presence of Lieutenant Waldheim in the organizational structure of the Heeresgruppe E staff commanded by General Loehr. Kurt Waldheim was not yet an official People's Party candidate for the Presidential election due to be held the following year but his name was being proposed with ever greater insistence in political circles in the capital.

Georg Tidl informed People's Party Secretary-General

Michael Graff, who refused to believe it. The major media were naturally not concerned with rumors spreading through the city. They were too busy reporting the accumulation of scandals which were beginning to damage the government's reputation internally, and the country's credit externally. The whole of Austria was buzzing at the time with the affair of wines which had been doctored with antifreeze, and about the Café Demel scandal. The owner of the most famous café in Vienna, Udo Proksch, had been found guilty of various frauds in which members of the government were heavily implicated.

At the outset of the Waldheim affair, the Socialist Party paid little heed to the accusations made against the former UN Secretary-General. In fact, although Waldheim had announced his candidacy under the banner of the People's Party, he had made contact with the Socialist Party with a view to becoming the sole candidate of the two major parties, thus foreshadowing the grand coalition between the Socialists and People's Party which was actually formed several months later, right after the general election held on November 23, 1986.

The Socialist Party was split between those who followed the line adopted by the political heirs of Chancellor Kreisky who were resolutely opposed to cooperation with the People's Party and those who, like the future Chancellor Vranitzky, saw a governmental alliance with the conservatives as the only way the Socialists could stay in power. They adopted the former course. So originally the Socialist Party resigned itself to fighting a campaign whose main aim was to limit the damage so that it would not be too weak when the time came to fight what it considered to be the decisive battle, the 1987 general election.

However, as the rumor about Kurt Waldheim's past continued to grow, the temptation increased in some party circles to use a new and unfamiliar weapon against Waldheim.

Chancellor Fred Sinowatz's friends began to ask themselves how best to exploit the accusations against the candidate Waldheim. It was very tempting to try and wrong-foot Kurt Waldheim's campaign which revolved around a single and unique slogan, "Vote for a man whom the world trusts!" From the Hungarian frontier to Lake Constance, this slogan covered the posters representing a smiling Kurt Waldheim. Standing with his wife Elisabeth, he wore traditional Austrian costume against a background of mountain scenery.

But it wasn't as simple as all that. There could be no question for the Socialist Party of a frontal attack on the personality of the opposition candidate. This would have involved carrying out a sort of cultural revolution within its own ranks, and especially destroying the complicity which had linked it historically with the People's Party in the joint resistance to the de-Nazification measures imposed by the Allies in 1945. The party strategists, sensitive as they were to the trends in Austrian public opinion, knew that it would be suicidal for the SPÖ to be responsible for a smear campaign which the majority of Austrians would utterly reject. "Woe to he who stirs up the mud which has swallowed up the black book of Austria's Nazi past!" seems to be the unwritten law governing the politics of the Second Austrian Republic.

Two factors forced the Socialist Party to abandon its reticence about Kurt Waldheim: the investigation conducted by Hubertus Czernin, a journalist on the weekly magazine *Profil*, and the intervention of the World Jewish Congress.

Journalistic Investigation, Public Campaign

*P*ROFIL is a news magazine run by a team of young reporters from an office in a blue-collar neighborhood of Vienna. Its 5,000 circulation owes much to its freedom of expression and the independence of its editorial line. Less sophisticated than the glossy but subtly aggressive *Wiener*, the magazine's style represents a sharp contrast to the Austrian daily press, whose conformity is as heavy-handed as a badly-made Viennese chocolate cake. The rumors about Kurt Waldheim also reached the office of Hubertus Czernin, a young journalist there. On February 21, 1986 at 11:00 AM, he got Kurt Waldheim's permission to consult his personal file in the National Archives. Astonished by what he found there, he asked for an interview with the candidate that very evening. Waldheim denied ever having belonged to Nazi organizations during his youth in Vienna.

On the morning of February 24, there was another meeting, more questions, and Kurt Waldheim admitted having served in the Balkans. "It was impossible get clear and coherent responses from him," Czernin recalls. "It was his persistence in lying that aroused the interest of the investigators."

On March 3, *Profil* published its first article about the Conservative candidate's past imperfect. The first piece to appear in the *New York Times* was published on March 4. Shortly afterward, the Yugoslav press took up the baton. Austrian and Yugoslav journalists shuttled between Vienna and Belgrade while the *New York Times* reported daily on the discoveries in the archives in Washington, and the European press conducted their own inquiries. One month later, on April 3, Kurt Waldheim announced his intention to start libel proceedings. He never did so.

Motivations of the World Jewish Congress

IT WAS not merely by chance that the World Jewish Congress (WJC) became involved in the electoral campaign. Officials of this institution founded in 1936 by Nahum

Goldmann were alerted to the rumors circulating in Vienna concerning Kurt Waldheim via two different channels, the *New York Times* and by Leon Zelman, the Congress's representative in Vienna. Leon Zelman is a former resistance fighter in the Lodz ghetto in Poland, who spent a total of three and a half years in the Auschwitz and Mauthausen concentration camps. After his miraculous escape from the death camps, he chose to settle in Vienna despite the curse hanging over the city for the Jews who lived through the black days of March, 1938. Despite all the objections he met with, especially in Israel, he set himself the mission of rehabilitating the Austrian capital in the eyes of the world in general, and the Jewish community in particular.

Supported by the Vienna city hall and the mayor, Helmut Zilk, he was put in charge of a "Jewish Welcome Service", an organization subsidized by the city, whose offices are located on the Stefanplatz, right in the heart of the historic area. His aim was to make the Viennese aware of its Jewish heritage. More famous Jews were born there than any other city in Europe, including Stefan Zweig, Arthur Schnitzler, Sigmund Freud and Gustav Mahler. Vienna owes a great deal of the intellectual and artistic enlightenment with which it was blessed at the turn of the century to Jewish citizens. Leon Zelman's patience and obstinacy gradually dispelled the prejudices which remained in Israel and the Diaspora against this city.

In this enterprise, he found an ally in the person of Israel Singer, a New York lawyer whose Viennese-born father had been one of those Jews forced to scrub the streets by the Nazis. Leon Zelman and Israel Singer organized the annual general meeting of the WJC in Vienna in 1984, despite the Jewish world's reluctance.

It was actually while the Congress was in session that the incident occurred which was to endanger the whole enterprise. This was the warm welcome given by the Minister of Defense to the Nazi war criminal Walter Reder. It was at Israel Singer's express intervention that the plenum did not interrupt its work, because most of the delegates wanted to leave the Austrian capital immediately in protest.

Israel Singer thus had ample reason to be interested in what was happening in Austria, especially as the other major activity of the WJC was the defence of the right of Soviet Jews to emigrate, and Vienna had traditionally been their first stopover in the West. Impulsive and strong-willed, a compleat New Yorker, Israel Singer seized on the Waldheim affair and turned it almost into a duel between himself and Kurt Waldheim. He chose a tactic which had once succeeded in causing the downfall of a world leader, Richard Nixon, who was put on the spot by two *Washington Post* journalists over the Watergate affair. The method consists of putting pressure on the international media to keep public opinion aware by concentrating on the issue and feeding the media new information daily.

In any case, there was no alternative. The Waldheim dossier was uncharted territory whose exploration involved research in locations very far apart, such as the Federal Archives in Washington, the Wehrmacht archives in Freiburg, West Germany, and the files of the Ministry of Foreign Affairs and the Ministry of Justice in Vienna.

The WJC hired a professor from the University of South Carolina, Richard Herzstein, to extract any items concerning Kurt Waldheim from the archives in Washington. His discoveries were published as soon as they were made.

Simultaneously, journalists from *Der Spiegel* in Hamburg, as well as various Yugoslav and Greek publications, conducted their own investigations. In Vienna itself, newspapermen on *Profil* and the Socialist Party's daily *Arbeiterzeitung* concentrated mainly on those aspects of Kurt Waldheim's biography dealing with his links to Nazi organizations during his student days.

This method had its advantages and disadvantages. It meant that the spotlight of news remained trained on the Waldheim case, but it meant that the investigators were forced to obey the laws of media dramatization. What the public were expecting was a definitive document representing conclusive proof that would catch Waldheim red-handed as a war criminal. In actual fact, the matter was more complicated than that and required deeper analysis and reflection, but this was hampered by the demands of the electoral schedule. For instance, the first revelations concerning Kurt Waldheim's Nazi past were published on February 21, 1986 by *Profil*, and repeated on March 4 by the WJC, less than two months prior to the first round of the presidential elections, and it wasn't until March 22 that the public was informed of the file about Kurt Waldheim which lay in the United Nations War Crimes Commission archive.

The counter-offensive by Kurt Waldheim's supporters, orchestrated by the Secretary-General of the People's Party Michael Graff, fully exploited the drawbacks in the tactics adopted by the WJC and its Austrian allies. Assisted by most of the Austrian press, especially the mass circulation newspaper *Kronenzeitung* and the financial daily *Die Presse*, Kurt Waldheim's campaign headquarters harped on the theme of an international conspiracy, in order to rally public opinion, which was all too willing to be convinced, around their candidate.

This counter-offensive was by no means devoid of anti-Semitic overtones. In his electoral speeches, Kurt Waldheim laid particular stress on the Jewish-sounding names of his main accusers. "It is not these gentlemen from New York, Singer, Steinberg and Rosenbaum, who will tell the Austrian people how to vote," he continually repeated at his public meetings, a statement which the crowd greeted with frenzied applause.

At the request of the Austrian President, Rudolf

Kirschläger, the WJC submitted the interim results of its research to him, while maintaining its public disclosures.

Simultaneously, Kurt Waldheim entrusted his son Gerhard with the preparation of a memorandum in his own defense. It was delivered to the Austrian President on April 12.

On April 22, Rudolf Kirschläger informed the country of his conclusions in a special television broadcast. In weighty and sententious tones, he first extolled his own virtues to Austrian public opinion, claiming that he had "halted the international press campaign directed against Austria during the Waldheim affair." As to the affair itself, he had forbidden himself the right to make any judgement, invoking his former calling as a judge to affirm "that in the present state of the case, no court would convict Kurt Waldheim." He concluded by saying "It is for the people to decide."

The cards were on the table. In the first round of the presidential elections, on May 4, Kurt Waldheim missed winning an absolute majority by a hair's breadth, but got 49.36% of the votes. A month later, on June 8, 1986, he won a landslide victory over his opponent Kurt Steyrer, and became the ninth Austrian head of state since 1918.

The WJC Did Not Have Unanimous Jewish Support

THROUGHOUT the controversy which pitted him against Kurt Waldheim, Israel Singer had to face attacks from the supporters of the former UN Secretary-General, which was quite natural, but he also had to contend with the skepticism—and even hostility—of a section of the Jewish world.

The reasons for the attitude of certain world Jewish leaders and of intellectuals is partly due to the nature of the WJC. As a central organization of Diaspora Jewry, it includes leaders of Jewish communities in the West and in the East, and has remained faithful to the spirit in which it was conceived by its founders, the American Rabbi Stephen Wise and Nahum Goldmann. The WJC has retained an independence of thought and action in relation to the State of Israel which has often displeased the leaders of the Jewish State, whatever their political affiliations. Its insistence in maintaining contact with the USSR and other Soviet bloc countries with the avowed objective of keeping communication channels open with Jewish communities in difficulty has contrasted with the hardline politics of many Israeli politicians, who are only prepared to talk to Moscow about one subject, that of Soviet Jewish emigration to Israel.

The over-cautious approach of the Israelis throughout the Waldheim affair caused some leaders whose communities were directly involved in Kurt Waldheim's past to exercise caution. This was the case, for instance, with the President of the Greek Jewish community, Joseph Lowinger, who expressed his doubts.

"I do not want to become Mr. Waldheim's advocate, but I have questions to ask myself." The Greek Jewish community did not hurry to investigate Kurt Waldheim's role in the deportation of the Jews of Salonika. Observers of the Greek political scene linked Joseph Lovinger's attitude with the normalization then in progress between PASOK (the Greek Socialist Party), the party in power, and the Jewish community, who disapproved of the rather pro-Palestinian stance adopted by Greek Prime Minister Andreas Panadreou in the Israel-Arab conflict. Eventually, Lovinger's community became one of the most active in the struggle against Waldheim.

It was the Jewish community of Austria which suffered the deepest trauma. The community has about 12,000 members and is run by a committee on which all political currents are represented. Most of the committee members tend to be conservative in outlook. Some of its better-known members, and especially Simon Wiesenthal, have never hidden their dislike of the Socialist Party, an animosity borne of differences of opinion with Chancellor Bruno Kreisky. The two men were constantly in court asking for damages for the insults they hurled at each other, the least of which was that of having collaborated with the Nazis.

When in early March, the WJC made its first accusations against Kurt Waldheim, the media naturally approached Simon Wiesenthal for his opinion, yet his initial reaction was to downplay the affair, claiming loud and long that he had no file on the former UN Secretary-General. This was important backing for the candidate Waldheim, who never failed to refer to Simon Wiesenthal's statements.

However, when he realized the kind of defense that Kurt Waldheim was putting up, Wiesenthal considerably altered his position. He distanced himself from Waldheim for good when the latter claimed never to have known about the deportation of Jews from Salonika. "That's all we had to talk about in the officers' mess!", he had claimed before hiding behind a wall of silence. Other Jewish community leaders managed to maintain a united front, for better or worse. The situation demanded it, and the Jews of Vienna worked hard to overcome their differences to confront the mounting anti-Semitism of public opinion.

Other personalities, known for their attempts to unmask former Nazis, also displayed reticence at the beginning of the campaign launched by the WJC. Since he was only a small cog rather than a big wheel in the Nazi machine, should Waldheim be condemned 40 years later? "I have always insisted on making the distinction between an active and a passive

Nazi," Serge Klarsfeld informed us at the beginning of the affair. As the proof accumulated, he abandoned his reserve and his wife, Beate, visited Vienna several times to take part in demonstrations against Kurt Waldheim. The very public nature of the WJC's campaign and its use of the media worried some Jewish community leaders. Yet were not these kinds of problems inevitable when a search for the truth was met with silence from all the countries involved?

If there were any need to be made aware that the remembrance of Nazi war crimes has for a long time been a political maneuver rather than a passionate search for the truth, the international reactions to the Waldheim scandal would be sufficient to prove it. Ever since the closure of the UN War Crimes Commission archives in 1949, this hotbed of compromising revelations has remained the private hunting ground of various secret police forces. In 1980, a researcher from New York University, Michael Palumbo, was actually barred from access to them by decision of UN officials. Kurt Waldheim himself, who had free access to this holy of holies during his term of office as Secretary-General, refused to open them up on at least two occasions on which requests were made in the proper manner.

As the journalistic and historical investigation into the Waldheim case proceeded, the government archivists showed themselves to guard their treasures ever more jealously. The federal Yugoslav government directly intervened to place an embargo on the Belgrade archives from the beginning of April. What were they afraid of?

Western Guilt

In all the major capitals, official inquiries were promised into the silent complicity which had accompanied Kurt Waldheim's career. Yet several months later, none had been completed. The British Minister of Defense, questioned in the House of Commons about the fate which Waldheim had intended for British and American prisoners of war, contented himself with promising to investigate the matter. In May 1986, the American House of Representatives, resorting to an exceptional emergency procedure, and the Senate, demanded the opening of a Federal investigation, the result of which caused the Department of Justice to ban Kurt Waldheim from ever setting foot on American soil.

The case of France is more disquietening. In 1979, the French military governor of West Berlin was asked to recover the personal file of an Austrian diplomat in the inter-allied archives of the city. This was done, but no trace has remained of the destination of this document. Seven years later, the private office of Prime Minister Jacques Chirac was thrown into a real panic when the question was raised again on the initiative of the Simon Wiesenthal Center in Los Angeles. The French Prime Minister's office and the French Foreign Ministry kept trying to palm the responsibility off on one other, while the French Ministry of Defence refused to comment.

A timid explanation was put forward unofficially. The measure taken in Berlin had been decided upon when the Austrian statesman was about to be awarded the Legion of Honor. Unfortunately, this award was made to him in 1961 when he was minister plenipotentiary, director of the Western countries section of the administration of the Austrian ministry of foreign affairs. Furthermore, the appropriate department in charge of such decorations has informed the authors that a detailed biography is never required when the Legion of Honor is awarded to a foreigner. Despite the promises of Jacques Chirac's spokesman, no explanation has been provided as to why France decided to start unearthing files in Berlin and thus put itself in the position of discovering that Kurt Waldheim had been lying for a long time.

The same official silence reigned even in the two countries directly involved in Waldheim's past. At first, there was no official word at all from Yugoslavia, it was simply noted that "nothing shall be done which will harm good neighbor relations with Austria."

On June 4, 1986, Greek Minister of Justice Apostolos Kaklamanis stated that as far as he was concerned he had searched the archives but "the names of Baldheim or Waldheim do not figure on our lists." The minister was making an amused allusion to a typing error in the telex from the Jewish organizations which had asked him to undertake this investigation. The negative result of this endeavour is, however, hardly surprising. Of the 1,235 judicial proceedings started in Greece from 1945 through 1953, concerning the 5,050 people suspected of war crimes. only 51 actually resulted in a trial and 31 verdicts were pronounced. All the files which had not been the subject of legal proceedings were pulped in 1975.

It should be added that the Greek secret services welcomed a number of former Nazi collaborators into their ranks after the liberation, and this was done with the blessing of the British who feared "communist subversion" above all. One can be sure that these people would have systematically cleared the files of any compromising material, if the State had not already done their work for them. It should be added that in March 1986, Austrian Minister of the Interior Karl Blecha visited Athens to meet with his opposite number, Menios Koutsogorgas and asked him to show moderation in the Waldheim Affair.

The general repugnance shown at revisiting the most troubled period in history was compounded by the influence of the personal relationships woven by Kurt Waldheim with many Western heads of state, especially among the conservatives. In the United States, where the WJC's campaign was at its most active, the reaction of President Ronald Reagan was awaited with curiosity. The President broke his long silence after the second round in the Austrian elections, granting media absolution to Kurt Waldheim who "had only done his duty."

The story behind this statement which appeared in the daily *USA Today* on July 2 is very significant. Shortly before this, the former US ambassador in Vienna, Helen Van Damm, went to Washington where she met with her old friend Reagan. Very much at home in conservative circles in Vienna, Helen Van Damm passionately defended Kurt Waldheim to the President, as she had done in many articles published in the Austrian press. She is not only a favorite of the American President, but also the wife of a Viennese financier and politician, Peter Gürtler, owner of the famous Sacher Hotel—and Chairman of the Kurt Waldheim electoral support committee.

Although the new US Ambassador in Vienna, Ronald Lauder, decided to boycott the investiture of the new President —for personal reasons (he is the son of the famous cosmetician Estée Lauder, who is Jewish)—Washington and Vienna were busy conspiring together. Kurt Waldheim actually took the initiative by telephoning Vice President George Bush in early April to request American neutrality in the matter. This conversation almost certainly had something to do with the sudden slowing down in the investigations conducted by the Attorney-General.

Official Congratulations and Plain Congratulations

As soon as the first round of the Austrian elections was over the Western governments breathed a sigh of relief. The Austrian people had approved of Kurt Waldheim. It would therefore be easy to hide behind "respect for national sovereignty" so as not to make any unfortunate slipups.

Only Luxembourg clearly demonstrated its disapproval.

In June, the authorities of that country and of Switzerland suddenly discovered that in 1944, the young Waldheim had presented a thesis supporting the idea of the annexation of the future Benelux countries and Switzerland into the Greater Reich. Explanations were demanded in Vienna, but this little convulsion of indignation was not pursued.

The Dutch government stated, for its part, that relations with Kurt Waldheim were sober. This sobriety was also sought by French president François Mitterand, who carefully weighed the terms in which his official message of congratulation was couched. In the opinion of the protocol experts consulted at the Elysée Palace, the telegram was worded "traditionally rather than cordially." The famous French cohabitation (between the Socialist President and the Conservative Prime Minister) was not applied in this case. While the national secretary of the Socialist Party, Jean Poperen, claimed to be "shocked" by the election of Kurt Waldheim, Jacques Chirac claimed "to have never seen any decisive proof of his responsibility for Nazi crimes." Others did not even wait for Kurt Waldheim's electoral victory to assure him of their hearty support. West German chancellor Helmut Kohl, for instance, an old friend of the Austrian Conservative, said even as early as April 27, 1986, "Waldheim is a great patriot. If I were an Austrian voter, I would know who to vote for." Curiously, this strong recommendation on how to vote did not shock those fierce defenders of "national sovereignty."

Yet it was the Kremlin that showed the greatest enthusiasm in learning of Kurt Waldheim's victory, not only over his electoral opponent, as might have been expected, but quite blatantly over "international Zionism." The eulogistic commentary issued by the Tass news agency was the first official reference to Kurt Waldheim for weeks. For the Soviet Union the affair had never existed.

The controversy surrounding the Austrian statesman

reawakened an East-West bi-polarization whose bitterness had tended to be forgotten. The Arab leaders, for instance, considered his election as a defeat for Israel, and thus for the United States. They fully agreed with the Soviet congratulations. Syrian President Hafez Al-Assad was the first to send his telegram of congratulation, closely followed by Colonel Muammar el Qaddafi and the Algerian Chadli Benjedid. Massoud Radjavi, leader of the Mujaheddin of the Iranian people, also congratulated him, as did Abu Nidal's group which devoted the first page of its magazine *Falastin wa-Thawra* to him.

The Egyptian press welcomed this "slap in the face for Zionism," and the PLO did the same. Shortly afterward, Waldheim was officially invited to Syria and Libya, but he was well aware, even though he did not fail to stress his "Arab friendships", that such visits would have had unfortunate repercussions in the West.

Were these Arab reactions a rejection of the specter of Western domination, a desire to accept at face value the opportunistic statements of the former Secretary-General, or were they examples of credulity when offered the theory of a "Jewish plot"? The Arab world's "Waldheim fan club" owes its existence to all these factors, but it is all the more surprising that Israel showed itself to be particularly reticent throughout the affair.

Israeli Fatalism

As the ultimate official Israeli reaction to Kurt Waldheim's election, the phrase used by Prime Minister Itzhak Shamir on June 11 resounds oddly today. "If the world decides to keep silent the hideous monster of Nazism could raise its head again." That Wednesday in the Knesset, the Israeli

Members of Parliament gave free rein to their indignation—for the last time. Emergency resolutions flowed toward Shlomo Hillel, the speaker. Dan Meridor, a member of the Likud Party and former secretary to Menahem Begin, took the floor, "Waldheim is a liar. He swore allegiance to Adolf Hitler and he served in the Wehrmacht, the Brownshirt army that prepared the Holocaust." Rabbi Meir Kahane tore up the red-and-white Austrian flag from the podium of the Knesset, shouting, "May the name of the cursed Nazi Waldheim be wiped off the face of the earth."

This memorable session of the Knesset subsequently proved to be little more than a psychodrama. Israel buried the Waldheim affair. Of course, the President of the State of Israel, Haim Herzog, did not send the customary message of congratulation to his new Austrian opposite number, his old colleague from the United Nations building in New York. But he wasn't the only one. Yet there was no break in diplomatic relations, just a simple recall for consultations of the Jewish State's Ambassador in Vienna, Michael Elitzur.

From the outset, the Israeli politicians did not seem to be interested or did not want to be. Shimon Peres hardly ever mentioned it. Eventually, he stated in June, "The problem is not to know whether or not he is going to be elected. No, the worrying aspect is the anti-Semitic undercurrent behind his election." It was not until Yitzhak Shamir, who took the reins of government over from him, reached New York, the home of the World Jewish Congress, that Shamir could be heard to revile Waldheim. "The election of such a man would be a tragedy." Haim Herzog, whose position as President of the State of Israel is more that of a figurehead than a politician, abstained from commenting. "I do not recommend taking any special measure if he becomes President of the Republic of Austria, I am not empowered to do so, it is up to the government to act as it sees fit." Presented as the great conscience of

Israel, Herzog preferred to remain more than discreet over the Waldheim affair. He considered that at the very most, and this may one day be held against him, that "Greece and Yugoslavia have observed a mysterious silence over the Waldheim affair."

Officially, the investigation continued. In fact, one wonders whether it was ever begun. In the weeks which preceded the final vote count on June 8, the Israeli press announced on several occasions that the publication of a report on the Waldheim affair was imminent. It was to be completed by Mr. Dennis Gouldman, Director of the International Department of the Ministry of Justice. It is still being prepared. The report has been put on the back burner. As for the Minister of Justice, Yitzhak Modai, who was forced by Shimon Peres to resign for his repeated attacks on the coalition arrangement with the opposition, his enthusiasm for this urgent case lasted for only a short time. Modai lamely hinted several times that Israel knew quite a lot about Kurt Waldheim's past, "He could be implicated, at least, in complicity in a crime," he said in late May. Then in early June, he started to retract, claiming out of the blue that he had no proof that Kurt Waldheim was implicated in Nazi war crimes.

Rather naively, Shevah Weiss, president of the parliamentary committee established to look into the Waldheim Affair, considered that Modai's statements were, "In complete contradiction to the efforts made by Israel." He insisted that an indictment be prepared against the former UN Secretary-General without delay, this being the first stage prior to a request for extradition. Itzhak Modai replied to us, through his secretary that, "At the time he had priorities other than the Waldheim Affair." And he even claims to have sent a "special envoy" to Europe to "enlighten public opinion about the personality" of the Austrian diplomat! No one ever saw this strange emissary, a certain Dov Schmorak.

The Israeli press, which also did not exert itself in

investigating Kurt Waldheim censured the faintheartedness of the politicians. "What a mess, these retractions. If it is true that Israel possesses proof against Waldheim, why is the government refraining from exposing them to the light of day before the citizens of Austria are called to the ballot box," asked *Yediot Aharonot*, the biggest Israeli daily, on June 8. For good measure, the newspapers raised the old cry of "This would never have happened under Begin."

Menaham Begin, the old charismatic leader of the Herut Party, now retired, has said nothing about Waldheim, although he knew him. It is true that in his day he publicly taunted the former West German chancellor Helmut Schmidt for having worn the uniform of the Wehrmacht. Although the Israeli leaders soon accepted Kurt Waldheim and rolled out the red carpet for him after his election as UN Secretary-General, Begin himself gave Waldheim the cold shoulder. Shortly after he came to power in 1977, Begin met Waldheim in the United States. He reported on this meeting immediately afterward, during lunch at the Waldorf Astoria in New York on Friday, July 22, 1977). "I talked to the United Nations Secretary-General about the plight of the Jews in Syria. Do you know what he replied? Mr. Waldheim told me that he would deal with it very soon." And the whole room burst out laughing at Begin's sarcasm.

"It must be confessed that our reactions never lived up to the expectations of the WJC and the Jews of the Diaspora," Abba Eban, chairman of the Knesset Foreign Affairs Committee and former Foreign Minister at the time when Kurt Waldheim was UN Secretary-General, told us. "Some people consider that Shimon Peres did not express himself strongly enough when speaking about the problem and that, on the contrary, he used language that was too cautious. Realism, and reasons of state dictate our reactions, and not only our feelings, it would be useless to deny it," continued Eban, who also considers it "useless" to insist that Jerusalem break off diplomatic relations with Vienna "We mustn't forget that 46% of the Austrians voted against Waldheim." Abba Eban does not deny that Israel reconciled itself to his election as head the United Nations.

"We knew that he had been an officer in the Wermacht, but we did not conduct any special investigations. We cannot be held responsible for the initial error. He had overcome every obstacle to get to such a position, and it is the so-called 'anti-Nazi' great powers in the Security Council who set the tone for the choice of such a person." Perhaps Abba Eban has supplied the key to the lack of interest in the affair shown by so many Israelis. It should be emphasized in this context that no major demonstrations have ever been organized in Israel to protest against Kurt Waldheim. "I believe the fact that he wore German uniform leaves us with no illusions. We had nothing to expect from a man with such a past." The Waldheim affair afforded Israel a measure of comfort in its belief, derived from Jewish fatalism, that, here again, there was not much to hope for from the great powers.

The Duty of Democracy

SINCE June 8, 1986, Kurt Waldheim has been the democratically elected President of a state which is one of the small number of countries where fundamental political liberties are respected, where there is a free press, and where universal suffrage is practiced under normal conditions. The chapter entitled "Austria" in the annual report of Amnesty International is one of the briefest, and is sometimes completely absent. Yet, the international community has been confronted with an unprecedented problem. It is faced with a head of state who has consciously tricked the whole world, who has won the confidence of the great leaders of this world on the basis of a falsified biography which exists thanks to universal silence on the subject.

As easy as it is, in the name of *Realpolitik*, to suppress one's prejudices against a bloodthirsty tyrant and receive him with all honors and in the name of the higher interest of the nation, it is equally awkward to diplomatically "manage" the presence of a Kurt Waldheim in the club of heads of state of democratic countries.

Visits of Presidents of the Republic of Austria to Western countries had passed almost unnoticed. The last visit to France, for instance, was paid by President Rudolf Kirschläger in 1985; it took place in a cordial and good-natured atmosphere. Austria, as a neutral country, tries to act as a bridge between parties in conflict, the East and the West, the North and the South, the Arabs and the Israelis. Even the conditions under which the presidential election took place will henceforward prevent the new Head of State from assuming this traditional role of messenger of good will, at least as far as the Western democracies are concerned.

The plaudits of the USSR and Arab countries such as Libya and Syria, who greeted Kurt Waldheim's election as a crushing defeat for international Zionism will do nothing to counterbalance the refusal of the Western countries—and especially the United States—to treat the new President of Austria like his predecessor. The very dignity of the democratic countries who have relations with Vienna is at stake. To treat Kurt Waldheim as if nothing had happened would be the same as agreeing that one had been deceived, or worse, it would add weight to the accusations of complicity which some people have not hesitated to level, though without convincing proof.

Kurt Waldheim relies on the natural tendency of countries to adapt to existing situations. "Don't worry!", he replied during his electoral campaign to those who were concerned about reactions abroad were he to be elected. "I know the international scene. Everything will return to normal once the libelous campaign that has been unleashed against me is over." Can Kurt Waldheim count on the cynicism of reasons of state?

There are at least two reasons why the democracies ought not to let themselves be caught in the protocol trap set for them by the occupant of the Hofburg, Austria's presidential palace. The first ensues from the nature of the Austrian consti-tution, which places the two first citizens, the President of the Republic and the Chancellor, on an almost equal footing. It is true that the former nominates the latter, but the Chancellor has the real power, since with parliament's approval he can   hold a referendum despite the opposition of the President. The latter represents Austria abroad, but in practice it is the Chancellor who conducts foreign policy. Boycotting Kurt Waldheim would not mean distancing oneself from Austria, provided normal relations were maintained with the Chancellor.

The present Chancellor, Frank Vranitzky, has actually exploited the handicap now suffered by Kurt Waldheim, by acquiring a fame and respect both in his own country and abroad which his predecessor, Fred Sinowatz, never had. Sinowatz found that Bruno Kreisky's shoes were too big for him.

The second reason which ought to stop the democratic countries from simply writing off the Waldheim case to the profit and loss account of their international relations balance sheet is of a moral nature. One of the foundations of the world order which emerged from the triumph over Nazism was the rejection by all the founder members of the United Nations of the basic values of the Third Reich. These included a belief in racial superiority, the priority of might over right, and the supremacy of the cult of violence. Kurt Waldheim has never been able to shake off the mud that has stuck to him, transported by the atmosphere of an era in which he always knew which way the wind blew. The right to rehabilitation and pardon has been recognized for those like him who were not heros. There are even former members of the Nazi Party, such as Karl Carstens, President of the German Federal Republic, who are honored without the whole world becoming upset by it. That is because, unlike Kurt Waldheim, Carstens has never tried to pull the wool over anyone's eyes and in his own way he has contributed to the work of self-reconciliation of a Germany which had admitted its guilt in the eyes of history. No, it is not the activities of Oberleutnant Waldheim that deserve to be brought to account but the constant insult to remembrance for which this champion of political opportunism is guilty.

The Canadian professor Irwin Cotler suggests in his conclusion to the report on the Waldheim case, "that a court be constituted consisting of judges from seven countries to investigate the basis for the charges leveled against Kurt Waldheim. Each country should designate an eminent jurist to preside over the court. The five countries which were the original members of the United Nations War Crimes Commission should take part in this court because for various reasons they all have an obvious link with the case. They are the United States, Canada, Great Britain, Greece and Yugoslavia. For this purpose, they should be joined by representatives of the German Federal Republic and Austria."

In the present state of jurisprudence concerning war crimes, the type of legal commission suggested by Professor Cutler, just like the extraordinary session of the Russell Tribunal which the present Chairman, the Yugoslav historian Vladimir Dedijer, tried to convene, could only conclude by drawing up a case file for a trial which could never take place, because according to all appearances Kurt Waldheim is protected by the statute of limitations.

A need for the truth, rather than a thirst for vengeance, ought to inspire such moves. For the Austrian collective conscience, an occasion would thus be presented for them to review their history which has been so manipulated that it has become unbearable. However, some observers in Vienna fear that for the younger generation, such a re-examination of the past would constitute the traumatic experience of a genuine "patricide." That is a very dramatic interpretation of the Waldheim case.

It is far more damaging for the collective conscience of Europe to live through the consequences of the scandal, namely, a victory for silence, despite pious assertions of a willingness for openness. On many occasions (though before he found himself assured of an electoral victory), Kurt Waldheim stated that he would willingly submit to the questioning of unbiased historians. Yet on July 13, 1986, Kurt Waldheim curtly responded to the Russell Tribunal that he would not accede to the request of "this privately-funded body." This reference to the material resources of an international commission clearly illustrates Kurt Waldheim's obsession with the idea of a plot. Didn't his supporters accuse the World Jewish Congress, without a shred of evidence, of having bought certain Greek evidence which was unfavorable to their candidate?

Kurt Waldheim thus came to believe in the theory according to which the controversy aroused by his case was a personal matter between himself and world Jewry. Never has anyone dared to use this argument with such insistence. Certainly, many of the investigators who are still trying to shed light on Nazi crimes are Jewish. The weight of contemporary history may be able to explain this phenomenon and the very specific relationship which Jewish tradition has with remembrance. To repeat the expression used by a Jewish community leader after a meeting with French Prime Minister Jacques Chirac about Waldheim: "It is often possible to pardon but never to forget."

The many Yugoslavs who have tried to correct the lies maintained by Kurt Waldheim were not Jewish nor was the Austrian writer, Peter Handke, who denounced Kurt Waldheim as "a cripple of the spoken word, master of the administrative verb."

The case of the new President of Austria brutally demonstrates how the Old World has grown senile. The subtle distinctions made by professional war-crimes hunters between "active" and "passive" Nazis have proved to be inadequate. The *Oberleutnant* was at best "actively passive" during the triumph of Nazism. The specific nature of Fascist brutality, denied in several pseudo-scientific theses, has become even more blurred in the ideological smokescreen thrown up by the confused and contradictory statements of the accused. Indifference has triumphed. Not one of the wealthy nations has voiced indignation. The accuracy of journalistic revelations is in reverse ratio to the collective emotion they have aroused. In the flood of congratulatory messages reaching the Austrian Presidential palace in June, 1986, one could almost hear the imperious command, "Silence, we are ruling!"

Postscript

Perhaps we shall never know whether within the closely-guarded secrecy of the *Alte Hofburg,* if Kurt Waldheim attempted to eradicate the sinister memory of the Kozara raids and the execution of hostages, events he knew about, even if he did not take an active part in them. What is evident, however, is that he never suffered from the scruples which tormented Gary Hart for a whole week. As soon as they knew of the sanctions imposed by the US Department of Justice, the Waldheim camp was put on the alert, their orders being to assume an air of indignation.

With his well-known pragmatism—which worked wonders when he was head of the UN—Kurt Waldheim has now understood that Edwin Meese's decision is likely to cause major cracks to open up in the Austrian consensus. Thus, it was as a politician, and not as a man stricken with remorse, that he appeared on television on April 28, 1987 to try once again his agile mixture of self-criticism and self-justification.

His self-criticism has been limited until now to an admission that he had "involuntarily underestimated" the impact of the revelations about his past. In this instance, Kurt Waldheim repeated yet again that he had "a clear conscience," and launched into a rather embarrassed explanation of the famous *Pflichterfüllung*—the importance of doing one's duty during the war. He repeatedly said this during his Presidential campaign. According to Waldheim, it was the fate of all the young men of his day to do their duty and serve in the *Wehrmacht,* and refusal to participate in the Nazi military adventure was an act committed by an infinitesimal minority. "I was not one of them," he concluded.

Might the decision of the US Department of Justice to keep him out have brought Kurt Waldheim back on the road to humility and repentance? That is unlikely. On April 25, 1987, exactly two days before the announcement of the American decision, he stated in the Brussels newspaper *Soir* that the publication by his administration of a "White Paper" about his past would finally put an end to all the controversy. He also refuted the argument that his attitude might have led to the diplomatic isolation of Austria. "I have had invitations from Western countries but I don't want to say which ones yet," he said mysteriously.

The isolation of Kurt Waldheim is very real. He was politely asked not to appear at the *Europalia* Exhibition in Belgium which was dedicated to Austria in 1987. His only consolations were the invitations from King Hussein of Jordan, Egyptian President Moubarak, and recently, Guatemala. As a further humiliation, when his cabinet and the People's Party pressed Austria's Chancellor Vranitzky to forego his official visit to the United States this May, or at least to bring a message of protest with him, Vranitzky replied that there was little hope the Americans could be persuaded to change their minds.

It was then, to everyone's surprise, that Kurt Waldheim received the support of John Paul II, who invited him to pay an official visit to the Vatican. Vienna was immediately triumphant. The newspapers that supported Kurt Waldheim were jubilant. In countries where the Pope represents the supreme moral authority, the unction of John Paul II is the equivalent of absolution and marks the calamitous defeat of the Austrian President's detractors.

Does this mean that the *Waldheim Affair* is over? World reaction, especially in the Roman Catholic world, shows to what extent the Austrian President still remains outside the cozy club of world statesmen. As soon as the news reached France, Cardinal Decourtray, Archbishop of Lyons and Primate of Gaul, expressed his sadness and dismay. Remember, the Pope's decision happened in the middle of the Barbie trial and profoundly shocked a prelate who was confronted daily with a litany of remembrance of genocide. He was moved to declare that he would react spontaneously to this development with Jewish sensitivity.

For what reason did John Paul II decide to endanger Judeo-Christian relations, when he'd worked so hard in this area? His recent visit to the synagogue in Rome, his unequivocal condemnation of Nazism and its attendant horrors during his trip to the Federal German Republic last May, his discussion over the vexed question of a Carmelite monastery in Auschwitz; all these did much to erase the ambiguous attitude to Nazism of his predecessor, Pope Pious XII.

John Paul II's smile, as he stood alongside a radiant Austrian President, was experienced by Jews all over the world as a slap in the face.

Was it through a desire for consistency in an *ostpolitik* which sees Vienna as an outpost for Christianity in confrontation with a Marxist, atheistic world? Or was it simply out of solidarity with a man who in his youth merely conformed to the pro-Nazi stance of the highest echelons of the Austrian Catholic clergy?

The Pope has not given any explanation—it is not part of the tradition—for his reasons for breaking the *cordon sanitaire*. Yet despite the symbolic importance of this gesture, world opinion didn't change.

Italy quickly made the excuse of political crisis to prevent Waldheim's visit to the Vatican to be accompanied by ceremonial visits with leading Italian statesmen. The more or less voluntary absence of many Western ambassadors to the

Holy See during the official ceremonies held in honor of Kurt Waldheim were, just like the demonstrations in St. Peter's square, a sign of mistrust.

However, it is in Austria itself that Kurt Waldheim's position has suffered most noticeably. In early June, the Viennese Section of the Austrian Socialist Party, the most important Section in the country, officially asked the President of the Republic to resign, despite the opposition of several party leaders, such as former Minister of Foreign Affairs Leopold Gratz and former Chancellor Fred Sinowatz. For his part, former Chancellor Bruno Kreisky asked Waldheim to make a personal move to re-establish his country's reputation.

Even more remarkable was the success of the commemorative vigil outside St. Stephen's Cathedral in Vienna, organized by members of the Austrian Resistance against Nazism. From June 8 through July 8, the anniversaries of the election and the assumption of office of President Kurt Waldheim, former resistance fighters, intellectuals, artists, and activists in the New Austria organization, initiated a dialogue with the local population in the center of Vienna. Passionate discussions were held in little groups until late into the night, during which young Austrians discovered those dark corners of Austrian history which had been concealed by official teaching from the very mouths of those who had lived through the period.

Elsewhere in the Hofburg, the official residence which once belonged to the Hapsburgs, Kurt Waldheim and his followers appeared deaf to the echoes of the slowly awakening Austrian memory.

Appendices

Chronology

November 10, 1918   Fall of the Austro-Hungarian Empire. Emperor Charles goes into exile. Proclamation of the First Austrian Republic.

December 21, 1918   Kurt Josef Waldheim born at Sankt Andrä-Wörden, near Tulln in lower Austria, first son of Walter Waldheim (original family name, Vaclavik), a schoolteacher, and his wife, Josephine, née Petrasch.

October, 1928   Walter Waldheim appointed school inspector in Tulln.

February 13, 1934   Attempted uprising by Social Democrats in Austria. Chancellor Dollfuss establishes the "Corporatist Christian State," better known as "Austro-Fascism." The democratic constitution is revoked, parliament is suspended and the Communist, Social Democrat and National Socialist (Nazi) Parties are banned, although the latter remains an active force in the country.

July 25, 1934	Dollfuss assassinated during an attempted coup and is replaced by Kurt von Schuschnigg, who continues his predecessor's policies. Rift deepens between anti-Nazi Catholics and those who favor alliance with Hitler's Austrian supporters.
June, 1936	Kurt Waldheim graduates from Klosterneuburg High School.
September 1, 1936– August, 1937	Kurt Waldheim volunteers for military service in the Dragoon regiment at Stockerau. During this period he decides he wants a career in the diplomatic service.
Fall, 1937	Kurt Waldheim begins his studies in Vienna at the Faculty of Law and the Consular Academy.
April 1, 1938	Kurt Waldheim joins the Nazi Students Association.
March 13, 1938	German troops enter Austria. Hitler proclaims the Anschluss, the annexation of Austria into the German Reich, a development welcomed by many Austrians. Walter Waldheim is jailed briefly for his anti-Nazi, pro-Austro-Fascism activities.
August 15, 1938	Kurt Waldheim is drafted into the Wehrmacht, the German Army, and joins a reconnaissance detachment of the 45th Infantry Division. He serves in the Sudentenland and France.

November 9/10, 1938	Kristallnacht—the full force of Nazi violence against the Jews and Jewish-owned property is unleashed in Germany and Austria, as the SA (the Brownshirts) loot and burn Jewish shops and synagogues.
November 18, 1938	Kurt Waldheim joins the SA. Also becomes member of the SA Cavalry Troop.
January 4, 1940– October 15, 1940	Kurt Waldheim takes a leave of absence from the army to continue his university studies.
December, 1940	Kurt Waldheim rejoins his unit in France.
Spring, 1941	Kurt Waldheim is sent to the Russian-Polish border.
December 17, 1941	Kurt Waldheim is wounded in the leg while serving in Byelorussia.
March 14, 1942	After convalescence, Waldheim is assigned to headquarters of Army Group E as liaison officer and interpreter (with the rank of lieutenant) and is stationed in Pljevlja in Yugoslavia. One of the missions of this unit, commanded by General Loehr, was to eliminate pockets of partisan resistance. (Loehr was later condemned to death for war crimes and hanged in Yugoslavia.)

November 1, 1943	In a bid to persuade Austria to defect from the Axis, the Allies issue the Moscow Declaration in which they call Austria the first victim of the Nazis.
July, 1943	Kurt Waldheim appointed second in command of Group Ia at the Wehrmacht command post attached to the Italian 11th army, and is posted to Arsakli, near Salonika, Greece. As an O3 Intelligence Officer, his duties including compiling daily intelligence reports, keeping track of prisoner interrogations and operations against partisans and civilians, and monitoring "special tasks", a common Nazi euphemism for torture and execution.
July-August, 1943	Over 40,000 Greek Jews are deported from Salonika to Nazi death camps.
August 15, 1944	Kurt Waldheim marries Elisabeth Ritschel, a member of the NSDAP (the Nazi Party) since 1938. His thesis on "Konstantin Frantz's Concept of the Reich" is accepted. (Frantz was a conservative Prussian statesman and notorious anti-Semite (1817–1891), who advocated a "Greater German Reich" as a western bulwark against the "Asiatic" power of Russia.)
Mid-October, 1944	Kurt Waldheim returns to his unit.
October, 1944– May, 1945	Brutal Nazi reprisals against Yugo-slavian citizens and partisans.

May 7, 1945	Germany surrenders unconditionally to the Allies.
May–August, 1945	Kurt Waldheim is interned in a camp at Bad Tölz, in Bavaria.
August 30, 1945	Kurt Waldheim presents himself at the Vienna Superior Court to be appointed "Referendar" (trainee lawyer).
November 26, 1945	Waldheim enters the Foreign Affairs section of the Austrian Chancellory. Inquiries about his activities during the war are cut short by officials of the Austrian Ministry.
December, 1947	Yugoslavia War Crimes Commission asks the Allied Commission for extradition of Kurt Waldheim for his part and responsibility in reprisals against villagers and partisans in 1944/45.
February, 1948	United Nations War Crimes Commission classifies Waldheim's file as "A" (having priority).
1958–1962	Kurt Waldheim serves as Austrian Ambassador to the United Nations.
1968–1970	Waldheim serves as Minister of Foreign Affairs in the People's Party government of Chancellor Josef Klaus.
1971	In an unsuccessful bid to become Austria's president, Waldheim is defeated by the Socialist candidate, Franz Jonas.

December 22, 1972	Kurt Waldheim is elected Secretary-General of the United Nations, as a compromise candidate between Eastern and Western blocs. He begins serving the first of two terms.
1982	Kurt Waldheim retires from the Austrian diplomatic corps.
September, 1985	First rumors of Waldheim's wartime past begin circulating in Vienna.
February/March, 1986	Austrian newsmagazine *Profil* publishes article on Waldheim's World War II activities. This is followed quickly by stories in New York, Yugoslavia, and elsewhere in Europe. The World Jewish Congress begins its investigation of Kurt Waldheim's files in the US National Archives.
June 8, 1986	Kurt Waldheim, in a landslide vote, is elected to a six year term as Austria's President.
April 27, 1987	US Department of Justice places Kurt Waldheim on a "Watch List" of undesirables, thereby denying him entry into America as a private citizen.
June 25, 1987	Waldheim meets with Pope John Paul II. It is his first trip outside of Austria since his election.

The Anger of Peter Handke

A NOVELIST, dramatist and poet, Peter Handke is an Austrian. He was born on December 6, 1942 at Writer, near Klagenfurt, at the time when his compatriot, Kurt Waldheim, was serving in the German army in the Balkans. In an article published in the magazine *Profil*, the author of *The Goalie's Anxiety at the Penalty Kick* and *The Left-handed Woman* cried out in rage on the eve of the presidential election which Kurt Waldheim was to win.

I would like to speak not as a writer, nor even as a citizen, I want to speak in the name of the real people of Austria, those who have so often been discounted, so rarely consulted, almost reduced to silence.

Kurt Waldheim will be a very different President from his predecessors, a hideous dwarf from the outset. This ghost from Transylvania whose portrait will adorn the classrooms and police stations, this cripple of the spoken word, master of the administrative verb, an amnesiac whose periodic addresses to the population are articulated by the hand which wrote so many "W"s at the bottom of sinister documents. His eternal indifference may at most influence a few like-minded people in a what will be claimed as a "mass movement", but he will never be able to share with the Austrian people the smallest spark of compassion for any victim.

Weak-eyed, he will offer our television viewers on his trips abroad only the two-faced dual portrait he owes to his past. Hard of hearing, he will be content to read on the lips of the visitors the platitudes to which he is accustomed, mechanically nodding his head with a beatific smile, and saying "I only did my duty", "War is war!", and shrugging his shoulders in disgust, "I have seen terrible things.", "I want to testify to gross injustice."

All we know of our candidate for supreme office is the way in which he expresses himself. It is only in this way that he is accessible to us today. His past, whatever it was, is justified today only by his terminology. It is useless to ask him to abandon it once and for all, this cannot be done because the way in which Waldheim expresses himself prevents any condemnation, despite our understanding of him. Waldheim's secret nature, which are reflected neither in his heart nor in his intelligence, are expressed solely in the diversity of his verbal conduct. We do not propose to judge his activity as a liaison officer during the illegal occupation of Yugoslavia by the German army, whose jargon described resistance fighters as "gangs." It is the orator of today whom we seek to judge, the man whose strategy, today and yesterday, consists of averting his eyes and blocking his ears. His principle? Let us wash our hands, because even if crimes were committed, there is no question of my bearing witness to them, because no rule exists that forces me to remember them.

Averting the eyes and blocking the ears enables one to be mistaken. Then there is nothing easier than to confuse a cry of pain with the creaking of a file cabinet. Seen out of the corner of an eye, the Jew getting into the boxcar could be mistaken for a sack of flour being sent to provision the front. In Salonika, in 1943, when the Jews of Greece were sent away—at their own expense!—with reduced fares for children and groups, to spend their exterminating vacations throughout Europe, Kurt Waldheim probably averted hs eyes. Just as he was forced to block his ears, in that same year, when recording a radio message in which a succession of expressions like "gangs," "gang activity," "support for gangs," "Jewish committee serving as a preparation center," "purge," before signing "Lieutenant Waldheim," preceded with the formula "certified copy." No protest would have prevented that, nor did it prevent him twenty-five years later in 1968 in Prague from signing the order to turn back the refugees.

No protest in the world could stop the election on June 8, 1986 of this hero, this royal specter, to the rank of head of state. Henceforward, the official documents of our republic will all be marked with a "W", just like the wartime documents and the order to send back the refugees from the Prague Spring. This time, it will not be the simple signature of an all-powerful notary, but the mark of Dracula on the sleeping body of the people.

Notes

1. Robert Musil, *The Man Without Qualities*, Martin Secker and Warburg Ltd., London, 1953. This multi-volume satirical novel is set in a mythical land called Kakania. The name is based on the letters "K u. K" which stand for *Kaiserlich und Königlich*, a title reserved for the Austro-Hungarian Empire. The book reflects Musil's contempt for the Austrian petty bourgeois mentality.
2. Michael R. Marrus, Robert O. Paxton, *Vichy France: Old Guard and New Order 1940–1944*, Columbia University Press, NY, 1982;
3. *L'Express*, August 29, 1986.
4. Interview in *Rolling Stone*, August 1986.
5. Kurt Waldheim, *The Challenge of Peace*, Weidenfeld and Nicolson, London, 1980; *ibid.*, *In the Eye of the Storm*, Weidenfeld and Nicolson, London, 1986.
6. Kurt Waldheim, *Un métier unique au monde*, interviews with Eric Rouleau, Stock, 1985;
7. The fortieth anniversary of Leo XIII's encyclical *Rerum novarum* was marked by Pius XI by his encyclical *Quadragesimo anno* issued on May 15, 1931. It dealt with social issues and condemned both individualism and collectivism.
8. D. Van Arkel, *Austrian Antisemitism*. Leyden, 1966.
9. *Le Monde*, May 4, 1986.
10. On the eve of the Liberation, a group of about one hundred resistance fighters was discovered at Tulln and shot.
11. In *Entnazifizierung in Österreich*, Verlag für Geschichte und Politik, Vienna, 1986.
12. George Clare, *Last Waltz in Vienna*, Macmillan, London, 1981.
13. G.E.R. Gedye, *Fallen Bastions: the Central European Tragedy*, Victor Gollancz, London, 1939.

14. Congressman Stephen J. Solarz had questioned Kurt Waldheim on November 26, 1979 about the claims made in the American magazine *New Republic* according to which he had falsified his past by erasing any compromising details.

15. Kurt Waldheim, *op. cit.*.

16. Two reports have catalogued and analysed the mass of archive material about Kurt Waldheim's military career. Firstly, there is the typewritten report, entitled *Pflichterfüllung, Ein Bericht über Kurt Waldheim*, which was compiled by historians sympathetic to the *Neues Österreich* movement, which opposed Kurt Waldheim as a presidential candidate. Published in Vienna in 1986, it has a preface by Peter Handke. Then there is the report prepared by the investigators acting on behalf of the World Jewish Congress (WJC), who produced a document entitled *Kurt Waldheim's Hidden Past, An Interim Report to the President of the World Jewish Congress*, WJC, New York, June 2, 1986.

17. The file "Waldheim Kurt" of the *Renseignements Archives WAST* handed over to the French military government of Berlin on March 21, 1979. Other sources mention a field hospital in the Orel region.

18. *Personalakt Dr Kurt Waldheim Aussenanmt, BMf Auswartige Angelegenheiten.*

19. File no. 23556 in the *Interallied Archives* in Berlin

20. Emile Guikovaty, *Tito*, Hachette, 1979.

21. Curiously enough, Kurt Waldheim's personal file in the Austrian Ministry of Foreign Affairs explicitly mentions "Serbokroatisch: gering" (Serbo-croat: a little), but no one seems to have asked themselves how he was able to acquire a smattering of that language while remaining quietly in Vienna until the German surrender, as he claims to have done....

22. *Kriegsrangliste*, Armeeoberkommando 12, June 30, 1942, Freiburg archives.

23. E. Guikovaty, *op. cit.*, p. 231.

24. See the newspaper *Start*, Zagreb, March 22, 1986.

25. See *To Vima*, Athens, March 13, 1986 and *Newsweek*, May 26, 1986.

26. Tito, *Complete Military Works*, Belgrade, vol. I, pp.128–129.

27. *Nuremburg Document 066 K*, December 16, 1942.

28. J. Vujosevic, *L'Occupation italienne*, in *Revue d'histoire de la Seconde Guerre mondiale*, PUF, No. 87, July 1972, p. 35.
29. See *Profil*, Vienna, March 10, 1986.
30. A. Kedros, *La Résistance grecque*, Robert Laffont, pp. 316–318.
31. H. Fleischer, in *To Vima*, Athens, April 13, 1986.
32. R. Herzstein, in *The Sunday Times*, London, May 11, 1986.
33. *United States National Archives*, Washington, vol. 311/181/0003-000.
34. M.I.D., U.S. War Department, *The German Military Intelligence 1939–1945*, Washington, pp. 224-225.
35. D. Kahn, *Hitler's Spies, the German military Intelligence*, Collier, New York, 1983.
36. *Libération*, April 18, 1986.
37. See Irwin Cotler, *Opening the file, the indictment of Kurt Waldheim*, Faculty of Law, McGill University, Montreal, 1986 (typewritten.)
38. Curzio Malaparte, *Kaputt*, Gallimard, 1972
39. The United States, Canada, Great Britain, Greece and Yugoslavia originally set up this commission.
40. See the excellent article by Jane Kramer, "Letter from Europe" in *The New Yorker*, June 30, 1986.
41. K. Gruber, *Von Breiung zur Freiheit*, Fritz Molden, Vienna, 1963.
42. Andrija Artukoviç was sentenced to death on June 3, 1986.
43. He never mentioned it in his main biography, V. Dedijer, *Tito Speaks: His Self-portrait and struggle with Stalin*, Weidenfeld and Nicolson, London, 1953.
44. V. Dedijer, *The Battle Stalin Lost: Memoirs of Yugoslavia, 1948–1953*, Viking Press, New York, 1971.
45. *The Jerusalem Post*, June 30, 1986.
46. Graham Greene, *The Third Man*, Heinemann, London, 1950.
47. Michael Berlin, *Baltimore Sun*, June 15, 1986.
48. A macabre anecdote illustrates this aspect of his personality. Accustomed as he is to ceremonial walkabouts, one day he approached a woman whose baby was visibly dying of malnutrition in her arms, and remarked distractedly, "What a lovely baby you have there!"